More
Activities
That Teach

More Activities That Teach

by Tom Jackson, M.Ed.

Red Rock Publishing

Credits
Cover Design: Bill Kuhre, Kuhre Ad Art
Page Design and Typesetting: Accu-Type Typographers
Printing: Publisher's Press

First Printing 1995
Second Printing 1997
Third Printing 1998
Fourth Printing 1999
Fifth Printing 2000
Sixth Printing 2001
Seventh Printing, 2003

ISBN 0-9664633-3-1

Additional copies of this book and other materials by Tom Jackson may be ordered from your supplier or from:

Active Learning Center, Inc.
3835 West 800 North
Cedar City UT 84720
(435) 586-7058 between the hours of 7:00 a.m. and 7:00 p.m. Mountain Time
Fax: (435) 586-0185
Toll free: 1-888-588-7078 between the hours of 7:00 a.m. and 7:00 p.m.
   Mountain Time

Web Site: www.activelearning.org

Have Tom Jackson speak to your organization or conference. Call for information.

Printed in the United States of America

CONTENTS

ABOUT THE AUTHOR
TOM JACKSON, M.ED.

Tom Jackson received his undergraduate and graduate degrees from the University of Southern California. He spent twelve years in the public school system in Southern California as a secondary teacher and coach. He taught in the Social Studies Department and coached both Boy's and Girl's Cross Country and Track. Tom has spent the last eleven years as a Prevention Specialist in Southern Utah. He directs the prevention/education programs for a public mental health/alcohol and drug center.

Tom wrote the highly successful book *Activities That Teach*, which contains sixty hands-on activities that help kids make positive life choices. He also edited a booklet called *Keeping Kids Drug Free: A Parent's Guide* and published a quarterly newsletter titled *Activities That Teach Update*.

Tom sits on the PK-12 Alcohol, Drug and Tobacco Curriculum Steering Committee for the state of Utah. He is also a member of the Utah State Substance Abuse and Anti-Violence Coordinating Council. He served three years as a national trainer for Just Say No International and is a trainer for the Federal Center for Substance Abuse Prevention. Tom is a nationally recognized conference speaker and workshop leader. His presentations have educated and entertained thousands of professionals and youth across the country.

ACKNOWLEDGMENTS

Thanks to all of the kids, teachers, youth workers and those individuals in the alcohol and drug prevention field, especially in the state of Utah, who have helped me create, try out and refine these activities. Without you folks, there would not be a second book. I also appreciate all of you who stopped me at conferences and workshops to comment on how you have successfully used the activities from my first book, *Activities That Teach,* and to offer ideas about new activities for me to consider. Your support and enthusiasm were key ingredients in making this second book a reality. Thanks again to my parents, Bill and Minola (better known as Dad and Mom), who gave me the start in life that has allowed me to pursue my dreams. I would like to make a special mention of my Dad who passed away before this book was published. He was always so proud of my first book. My most heartfelt appreciation and love goes to my wife Janet. She has shown a lot of patience and long suffering while listening to new ideas, making suggestions and then helping to proofread what I have written. Thanks also to my kids Frank, Brent and Denise who helped advise me as to what would work and what wouldn't. A special thanks to my older son, Frank, who was my computer advisor and helped to proofread many of the activities and chapters in this book. My final thanks goes to God, who has seen fit to bless me in this endeavor and to surround me with a wonderful family and supportive friends.

INTRODUCTION

I work with many kids who have glazed over eyes, bored expressions on their faces and an attitude that says "Go ahead and try to teach me something!" These are the very people that drove me to start using an active learning approach to alcohol and drug prevention in the first place and later to many other self-management life skills that kids need to succeed in today's complex world. My first book *Activities That Teach* shared this same active learning technique with thousands of others who work with kids. For those who have found the active learning teaching strategy to be effective, this second book gives you more of the same user-friendly activities that you have grown to love.

Thank you one and all for your support and words of encouragement as I have traveled around the United States giving workshops and participating in conferences. These have been exciting opportunities for me to explore with you the active learning model and various activities in a hands-on format. I have also appreciated the activities and variations that you have shared with me.

In this book I have expanded the opening chapters with new research information and insights gained over the past few years from my own personal experiences. The opening chapters are still included for those who do not have a copy of *Activities That Teach*. Two completely new chapters have been added in response to conversations I have had with those of you who have been using my activities. The new chapters deal with discussion problems and methods you can use to divide your group into partners and teams.

I hope you enjoy these new activities as much as I have and find them to be equally as fun, practical, educational and motivating as those in my first book. If you have any suggestions or comments please feel free to give me a call or write. I am always glad to talk with others who are also "in the trenches" trying to help our children and youth as they move towards happier and more productive lives. With that . . . it is on to *More Activities That Teach*!

Chapter One

What is Active Learning?

"For most students academic learning is too abstract. They need to see, touch and smell what they read and write about."

John I. Goodlad

For the past twenty-three years I have been a part of the educational system in the United States. For twelve years I was involved as a public school teacher and the last eleven as a Prevention Specialist working with youth issues such as alcohol, drugs, tobacco, sexuality, depression, family conflicts, runaways, suicide, etc. I have seen thousands of kids in hundreds of classrooms across the country. I have determined that the education system knows how to transfer facts from teacher to student, but I have also noticed that in the more abstract area of life skills we fall short. Life skills such as communication, problem solving, decision making, interpersonal relationships, values formation and healthy lifestyle choices are being presented in such structured curriculum that our students are turning a deaf ear.

I believed very early in my educational career that we needed to help our kids in the area of life skills if they were to succeed in society. To do this effectively, I found myself frequently using non-traditional approaches. The traditional lecture, worksheet, review and test format was not impacting behavior the way I wanted. Research has shown that teachers do about 80% of the talking in most classrooms; no wonder it is said that if you want to really know something, you should teach it. I however, wanted my students to have to think for themselves and draw conclusions from their own thought processes, not from mine. It was after reading Edgar Dale's research concerning learning and retention that I really started researching and formalizing my approach to teaching beyond the three R's. The result was creating, collecting, adapting and refining a number of lesson plans that would impact kids. This search led me to Active Learning, a hands-on teaching strategy that shifts the spotlight from the teacher to the students.

Active Learning is a concept rather than a true educational model. It can combine a number of different models within it and jump back and forth between them with great ease. Active Learning has people participate in their own learning process by involving them in some type of activity where they physically become a part of the lesson. Simply put, it's learning by doing. Examples of this would be role-playing, simulations, debates, demonstrations, problem solving initiatives, skits, video productions, discussions, games, etc. Two teaching techniques that fit into this concept are Cooperative Learning and Experiential Learning. Both of these involve the learner as an active participant in the educational process.

Active Learning is based on a process rather than an outcome. What is learned as the activity takes place is as important as any of the facts that are an outcome of the activity. It is the interaction among the students that bring this learning about. Patricia and Timothy Greene wrote in their book, *Substance Abuse Prevention Activities for Secondary Students,* "An important fact about the process approach is that the skills that are taught are transferable to other tasks. Process skills are not isolated bits of knowledge, but broad skills that can be used for a lifetime." Active Learning is an effective tool to teach not only information, but lifelong living skills. Through the process, an individual can internalize information and assume responsibility for their decisions regarding personal lifestyle choices.

Active Learning has some aspects of left and right brain research in it. The lesson plans that are incorporated into this book are definitely set up that way. The first part of the lesson is logical and feeds the left brain with an introduction of facts, thereby giving the students some basic knowledge to work with. The second part of the lesson is very right brain: You reinforce that knowledge and allow for an understanding of it's importance by involving them in an activity. Many people assume that fun and learning can't occur at the same time. This is simply not true. By using an approach that utilizes fun, learning is not automatically eliminated. Some people equate a quiet classroom or a well behaved student with learning, but observations have shown us that kids may just be day dreaming while you are talking. Even the memorizing of answers to test questions can occur without any real impact being made on their thinking processes.

The right side of the brain involves more of the emotional faculties of the brain. Physical movement and the varied assault on the body's senses helps to imprint the activity on the student's brain. After completion of the activity you shift back again to the more logical left side of the brain. The process that took place during the activity is reinforced through a processing or discussion time. The students talk about what took place and the importance of the interactions. The whys and the hows can be explored during this time. Then the students discuss how the activity can be applied to their lives. It is during this discussion time that the students can transfer what they have learned from the activity to their own lifestyle.

Let me caution those of you who are thinking, "This sounds neat but I can't do it in my class." I do not advocate the use of Active Learning as the only teaching technique that you use in your class. It is but one of the tools that you can have at your disposal. Used properly, Active Learning can help you in a variety of ways to teach information that is difficult to transmit via other formats. I agree that if used exclusively this or any other method of teaching would lose it's appeal and effectiveness. I also caution you however, not to discard this technique just because it is different from what you have been using or because it sounds like too much fun.

Active Learning Process

1. **General concept is presented to the group.**

2. **Specific information concerning the concept is received by the group.**

3. **Activity is undertaken by the group.**

4. **Group explores actions and consequences during the activity.**

5. **Group discussion is held immediately following the conclusion of the activity.**

6. **General principles are discussed.**

7. **Specific life applications are derived from the general principles.**

8. **Life applications are internalized by individuals according to their needs and readiness.**

9. **Students act on what they have learned.**

While this is Active Learning at its best, you must realize that Active Learning is like an adventure. You can not predict exactly what will happen. What you can be sure of is this: Whatever learning does take place will be significant to those involved; they will own what they learn and will retain that knowledge for a longer period of time than through any method of passive learning that we have discovered yet. It is the process that makes Active Learning the teaching tool that it is, and this process has a synergistic quality about it, meaning what comes out is greater than what goes in. I hope you enjoy watching your students explore the world of decisions, consequences, emotions and opinions through the use of Active Learning.

Chapter Two

Importance of Active Learning

"The only learning that really sticks is that which is self discovered."

Carl Rodgers

A great deal of research has been done into the way people learn. One fact keeps repeating itself over and over again and that is people who are involved in their own learning process will understand more and remember the information to which they were exposed for a longer period of time. Howard Hendricks in his book *Teaching To Change Lives,* stated it this way, "Maximum learning is always the result of maximum involvement." It is involvement that seems to be the key.

The truth is, students of all ages love being actively involved in their learning. Active Learning allows people to become involved in their education. This involvement can occur through role playing, simulations, games, discussions, demonstrations and problem solving initiatives. In the book *Creative Teaching Methods,* Marlene LeFever puts it this way, "Participation in the learning process stimulates learning and encourages growth. When children and adults participate in the learning process, truth becomes real in their lives."

We talk about teaching values and attitudes, but few teaching techniques allow us to really affect the inner mind of people. This is one of the important factors of Active Learning. It is a teaching method which allows students to transfer facts into behavior.

People do not succeed by information alone. The education system has recognized this fact for some time now and has been aggressively teaching life skills, living skills and social skills for the past several years. Active Learning uses many approaches to address these skill areas and apply that knowledge to the lives of individuals. It's effectiveness is recognized in *Games for Social and Life Skills* by Tim Bond. He states, " . . . games offer the participants structured experiences that are particularly suitable for improving social skills. The structure of the game can focus the experience on specific issues. In addition, learning by direct personal experience has far more impact than being advised on the basis of someone else's experience, which is inevitably second hand. First hand experience makes it easier for someone to relate to whatever they have learned from the game and apply it to everyday life."

Another author, Spencer Kagan, in his book *Cooperative Learning* points out the benefits of participatory learning in the area of self esteem. He states, "Almost all studies which compare the self-esteem of students following cooperative and traditional interaction, show significant gains favoring students in cooperative classrooms."

Helping kids to succeed after graduation means giving them the skills necessary to communicate and interact with others. John D. Rockefeller was quoted as saying, "I will pay more for the ability to deal with people than any other ability under the sun." This thought is reinforced by one survey which determined that the most common reason people are fired from their first job is not what they know, but rather their inability to relate with others on the job. Even with this knowledge, traditional teaching methods consistently emphasize information at the expense of interpersonal skills. David Johnson, in his book *Cooperation In The Classroom,* states, "grades in school do not predict which students will have a high quality of life after they graduate. The ability to work with others does."

Active Learning can provide a vehicle for the teaching of these interpersonal skills while still covering material that is basic in any educational system. These interpersonal skills are not only important in the work place, but in all areas of our lives, whether it be our job, marriage, community or relationships. This teaching technique allows a variety of ways to foster communication skills, higher-level thinking skills and social skills. These are skills which are in demand no matter what area of life you wish to discuss.

No longer can we sit back and give book knowledge without rounding out the educational process with skills that allow our graduates to participate in our increas-

ingly complicated and interdependent society. These
skills are not easily taught nor easily learned. This difficulty is exactly why the use of Active Learning is
important. It allows the student to practice these skills
while in the safe confines of a classroom and with the
guiding hand of a teacher.

Advantages of Active Learning

1. **Students are motivated.** The approach has a cer-
    tain amount of fun included in it. Fun is a motivat-
    ing factor for kids. It is easier to teach kids when
    they think they are enjoying themselves, even if the
    fun involves learning. Just by doing something that
    is a little different, kids become motivated to par-
    ticipate.

2. **Takes place in a safe environment.** The class-
    room is a place where experimentation and failure
    should not only be allowed, but encouraged. With-
    out risks being taken, real learning comes to a halt.
    The teacher can provide that safe environment
    through modeling and setting acceptable limits of
    behavior in the classroom. This would include rul-
    ing out name calling, singling out individuals for
    ridicule, sarcasm, and other degrading behaviors.

3. **Participation by the entire group.** Being
    actively involved means that the students are part
    of the lesson plan. Information is not given to them;
    they go after it. This is a "get up and go" type of
    learning that places everyone in a position to bene-
    fit from being a part. Some activities require
    strength; other activities require brains, and still
    other activities simply require a person to be a part

of them. Everyone finds a place and contributes in his/her own way.

4. **Each person takes responsibility for his/her own learning.** As a participant in the Active Learning process, the students must make their own assumptions and decisions about what is taking place. Others can tell them what to think, but each person is responsible for deciding if that reasoning is right for him/her. This is the challenge of an Active Learning model. No one has the right or wrong answer, each person can interpret the action for themselves and apply it to his/her own circumstance.

5. **It is flexible and thereby relevant.** The same activities can be used with a wide range of age groups. Some of the rules or language may have to be changed when sliding up and down the grade levels, but the basic activity can remain essentially the same. By making changes you can make an activity relevant to a wide variety of age groups while still exploring the same concepts. Age or developmental appropriateness is easily accomplished through variations and adaptations which can be made by the teacher.

6. **Receptiveness is increased.** Many topics when approached through traditional teaching models are automatically tuned out by kids because they feel "preached to." By using an Active Learning approach where the principles and application of those principles are expressed by the kids themselves, the information becomes easier for them to hear and apply.

7. **Inductive reasoning is stimulated.** Answers are not given, but rather explored. Questions must be asked and answered before the activity can be completed. Many of the questions and answers come from the students themselves during the course of the activity. Kids will use trial and error to move through many of the activities. It will be during this discussion of ideas and the subsequent processing, that much of the learning will take place.

8. **Participants reveal their thought processes.** While the activity is taking place and during the discussion after the activity, the teacher is able to determine the level of student understanding. The teacher can now concentrate his/her teaching in the areas of greatest need. The key is to listen to what the students are saying. Their words are a window into their minds. Too many of our teaching techniques emphasize the instructor doing so much talking that he/she never gets to hear what the students are thinking other than the required responses during question and answer time; Active Learning allows you to hear them as they think, decide, act and process different situations that you place them in.

9. **Allows for the correction of failure.** In real life when we make a mistake it is hard to go back and replay the tape of life and correct it. In an activity format, if you make a mistake that results in failure you can stop the activity, discuss other options and start over again. Barriers and dead ends become "teaching moments" where the class learns that mistakes can be beneficial and lead to something better, rather than failure being the end of trying.

10. **Allows for greater risk taking.** Kids feel free to participate and learn through involvement because they know the activity is not real. Taking risks is hard in a society that idolizes winners and throws away losers. When we see an Olympic athlete who has finished second being asked why he didn't get the gold, you know that winning is everything. By allowing students to participate without the stress of having to win, you give them the freedom to try without the disgrace of failure.

Chapter Three

Why Use Active Learning?

"Knowledge cannot be passed like a material substance from one mind to another; for thoughts are not objects which may be held and handled . . . Ideas must be reexperienced."

John Milton Gregory

Much of the teaching that we do today is outcome based; we are looking for the learner to acquire a certain set of facts or body of knowledge. This has manifested itself in the significant growth of multiple choice testing, which is being used almost exclusively in many classrooms. While this type of testing has a place in education, it needs to be balanced by teaching students that the process in which they arrive at answers can be as important for their future success as the answers themselves.

Some people are asking the question, "Which is more important, to have students learn the outcomes of previous reasoning or to have students learn the skills to conduct their own research?" I feel that both strategies have their usefulness, but we have placed too much emphasis on the former and not enough on the latter. In the book *Cooperative Learning* by Spencer Kagan, he states "Exclusive study of the products of prior work looks back, disempowering students, conducting creative investigations looks forward, empowering students." It is this empowerment of the student that we wish to encourage through Active Learning.

If we want learning and problem solving to be a continual and lifelong process which will result in changes of attitude, values and beliefs, then we need to emphasize process over content. We are an information society. Presently the rate of new information, especially in the scientific and technical fields, doubles every two years according to Elizabeth Christopher in her book *Leadership Training Through Gaming*. She also concludes that this rate will continue through the end of the century.

When we lock our students into memorizing strictly content or understanding hypothesis developed by others, we have relegated them to proving the past but not developing the future. Active Learning through such exercises as role playing, simulations, initiative problems, games, demonstrations, and discussions provides a great opportunity to teach process. Active Learning allows people to learn from the inside out in a four step process. The first step involves experiencing feelings during the activity. The second step is to use inductive reasoning to work through the activity and complete it. The third step involves discussing what happened during the activity, and the fourth step is to apply what was experienced and observed during the activity to general and personal situations.

Active Learning is a technique which allows students to become more directly involved in their education. In their book *Do It! Active Learning In Youth Ministry* by Thomas and Joani Schultz, they state that "Studies reveal that the more students become involved in an experience, the more they'll learn from it." In addition, research has shown that kids are more motivated to learn when they are active participants in their own learning process. Part of this learning factor is in the format of Active Learning itself; students are able to get immediate feedback during the activity from others involved in the same activity. With teacher guidance, peers are teaching peers to solve problems and overcome artificially created barriers. As an added plus, the students find Active Learning to be a fun way to learn. This increases their willingness to be involved and some learn in spite of themselves.

Marthea Falco, in her book *The Making of a Drug Free America: Programs That Work*, looked at what really works in the area of prevention. She gathered research from across the country and discovered that five key elements appeared repeatedly in successful school-based prevention programs. Here are the five ingredients that she found in common.

1. Teaching credible information is very important.

2. The myth that "everyone is doing drugs" must be exposed.

3. Children must be taught practical strategies for resisting drugs.

4. Students must be actively involved in the learning process.

5. Family and community need to participate in the prevention effort.

I would like to expand on number four. Malthea Falco's research concluded that programs which simply lecture to kids or rely on filling out worksheets, do not make much of an impact. Students need to be involved in role playing, discussion, simulated experiences and other active learning strategies to help them internalize concepts.

Another study of 6,000 students which was conducted by Cornell University Medical College's Institute for Prevention Research points to the success of skill building as an effective prevention tool. The study found that programs which focus solely on factual information surrounding the dangers of drugs are not effective in reducing drug use. It also found that the teaching of resistance skills has a positive short-term effect, but needs to be repeated periodically. The most effective prevention programs were those that focused on general life skills such as goal setting, decision making, friendship-making, critical thinking and others. The conclusion of the survey was that skill building works. By using Active Learning you are able to teach these skills in a non-threatening, effective manner. You are able to move from "preaching to teaching."

Through the use of activities, combined with processing, your students will be gaining the skills and information they need to remain nonusers of alcohol, tobacco and other drugs. These same skills will also help them to avoid other self-destructive behaviors such as suicide, sexual activity, violence, gang membership, depression, etc. Remember that repetition is vital in prevention.

Just because you have taught a concept once doesn't mean that your kids have internalized it. Activities are an excellent way to repeat and reinforce your message.

Active Learning can also be used to keep your curriculum fresh, exciting and non-repetitive. It is best used to supplement, add to and embellish traditional programs rather than replace them. It creates a learning environment that is more complex, more engaging, less predictable and less static than the traditional classroom approach. This approach has been able to combine periods of activity with structured group reflection and personal evaluation to enhance one's knowledge base and motivate behavior change.

Retention is a key component of learning. If you take a look at Professor of Education Edgar Dale and his "Cone Of Learning" research on retention, you will find which teaching techniques produce a higher percentage of retention. His research at Ohio State University measured the degree of effectiveness each teaching technique had on retention. He found that students will remember five to fifteen percent of what they read or hear, ten to twenty percent of what they see, and forty to fifty percent if the information is presented both visually and verbally. A good example of this would be television programs or movies. We receive input both verbally and visually in both of these mediums. People will be able to describe to you scene by scene what they experienced at the movie theater for weeks after attending. If discussion is the teaching technique, then students will remember up to sixty to seventy percent of what was discussed. However, the highest retention rate (up to ninety percent) involves personal experience. Active Learning combines all of the aforementioned teaching techniques: Students hear information; they see the activity take place; they are involved in a follow-up discussion, and in most cases, they personally experience what takes place.

In a recent (1994) meta-analysis done by Dr. Nancy S. Tobler, a comparison was made between the effectiveness of interactive and noninteractive programs. Interactive programs emphasized interaction and exchange of ideas among peers, and encouraged active participation of all students in the classroom. Noninteractive programs had program content taught by the teacher in a didactic manner. The areas that Dr. Tobler examined were knowledge, attitudes, social skills and drug use. The results are expressed in percentage of change.

	Interactive	Noninteractive
Knowledge	53%	16%
Attitudes	33%	6%
Social Skills	76%	8%
Reducing Drug Use	18%	8%

Looking at the differences in percentage of change between interactive and noninteractive methods, I think you will agree with me that the choice is obvious. The interactive teaching method achieved superior results in all four categories that Dr. Tobler researched.

Active Learning also addresses the needs of different types of learners. A lot of research has been done on the different ways that people learn. Every class or group will have a number of each type of learner. The main groups of learners are visual, auditory and kinesthetic. Each group is classified by which sensory stimuli they prefer when acquiring new information. Each classification classifies which type of stimuli is preferred and most effective for that particular group. Visual learners perform best when they can see new information as it is presented to them. Auditory learners absorb information through the spoken word. Most teachers fall into this category; they enjoyed school and found it to be a pleasant experience since most of the teaching done in today's school system is through auditory techniques. Because of this pleasant experience, they chose teaching as their profession. Kinesthetic learners are those that learn through touch or movement. Kinesthetic learners are most often male and many times, lower achieving students. The low achievement logically follows, as physical involvement is the least used technique in our schools. This group makes up a large percentage of the student population, yet the most effective teaching technique is almost totally ignored except in classes such as shop and physical education. Active Learning allows all three groups to use their particular talent in the learning process. Rather than favoring one group over another, it combines all three. This is why the technique is so successful, even with high risk students.

Teachers can use Active Learning for a number of outcomes. David Johnson, in his book *Cooperation In The Classroom*, states that this type of learning "should be used when we want students to learn more, like school better, like each other better, like themselves better and learn more effective social skills." I think that any teacher would want to see these outcomes in their students. Active Learning can be used to confirm, modify or refute prior beliefs. It gives the teacher a perfect vehicle to create a climate for student growth in areas that are hard for teachers to impact through many traditional teaching models.

Benefits of Active Learning

1. Active Learning involves everyone in the group.

2. Active Learning is student oriented, not teacher oriented.

3. Active Learning is process, not outcome oriented.

4. Active Learning is reinforced and directed through a discussion time.

5. Active Learning allows teachers to observe their students as they interact with each other.

6. Active Learning puts the burden of learning where it belongs - on the students themselves.

7. Active Learning allows students to have fun while they learn.

Chapter Four

Overcome Objections to Active Learning

"If teaching were only telling, my children would be incredibly brilliant; I've told them everything they need to know."

Howard G. Hendricks

There are always a lot of reasons not to do something different. Just the mere thought of trying something new is enough to cause some people to become nervous. Fortunately, Active Learning is not a radically new idea nor is it revolutionary in the education field. The reason I say fortunately, is because really new ideas regarding education take years and sometimes decades to become accepted. Since Active Learning has its base in Cooperative Learning, Experiential Learning and a number of other learning models, it can not really be called new. Many teachers have been using the ideas expressed in this book for some time. However, there are still a large number of teachers who choose not to experiment with anything that is different. Hopefully, their attitudes can still be changed.

I am not advocating throwing out the teaching strategies that you are now using. Active Learning activities are designed to supplement the traditional classroom approach. These activities are not intended to replace what has been taking place in the classroom, rather they are an additional tool for the classroom teacher or group leader. Many people believe you must take an either/or stand. That is not necessary. Traditional approaches can be easily combined with Active Learning techniques.

Active Learning does leave the teacher with a more complex, less predictable and, in some cases, a less familiar style of teaching. No longer can the teacher be sure of what the outcome of a lesson will be. The activity itself, the interests of the students and the needs of the group will drive much of the discussion. Some teachers and group leaders are uncomfortable with such an open approach. These individuals try Active Learning once or twice and then abandon it for the more familiar and structured confines of worksheets, lectures and reports. However, I feel that through careful structuring of the activity and skillful directing of the discussion, you can accomplish your desired objectives. Don't make an either/or decision; instead use a variety of teaching methods to reach your students.

Active Learning is simply another tool in the teacher's arsenal to attack the apathy that most students show for school. Notice I don't say learning. You can take a student who seems down right hostile towards education, put that student in a situation where he/she wants to learn something of interest to them and they will work with great enthusiasm until they have mastered that area of interest. One example would be the football player who can't remember to do his homework but can memorize his blocking assignments for up to a hundred different plays. In the book *Cooperative Learning* by Spencer Kagan, he states that "learning is best promoted by being motivated to learn and being in a situation which allows learning to occur." Active Learning helps in both of these areas. The motivation for learning comes from the fact that the method of instruction has a fun side to it. Students want to participate in the lesson activity. The activity is also the vehicle by which the student is in a situation which allows learning to take place. It replaces passive learning with learning through involvement.

Active Learning is also a great vehicle to encourage interaction between your students. It is difficult not to be involved in the activity and with your fellow students when the success of your group depends on what you do and what happens between the members of the group. It is through this very interaction that learning takes place. It is learning that goes beyond the curriculum and into areas that affect the very being of your students and their success in life. In the book *Cooperation In The Classroom* by David Johnson, he relates that "extensive research comparing student interaction patterns clearly suggests that cooperation among students produces higher achievement, greater motivation to learn, more positive relationships among students, greater acceptance of differences, high self-esteem, and a number of other outcomes." Surely these are some of the outcomes that you would like to see in your students.

Another factor that research has shown is the fact that youth problems such as drugs, alcohol, teen sexual activity, suicide, etc., can not be dealt with in isolation. Prevention efforts in these areas must focus on people and the underlying factors that influence these types of behaviors. Active Learning deals with many of the underlying factors that have been shown to contribute to these areas of concern. These factors include communication skills, problem solving, formation of values, working together, goal setting and others. Many of the above listed acting out behaviors are a result of kids trying to clarify their uniqueness and discover what works for them. Patricia and Timothy Gerne, in their book *Substance Abuse Prevention Activities of Elementary Students*, state that "by the fourth grade other sources of information from peers, television and older siblings begin to challenge parents as the sole authority. Children, therefore, will need to learn necessary skills to clarify their own value judgments."

It is through lesson plans that utilize such techniques as Active Learning that your students will be able to analyze exactly what they believe. We know that "scare tactics" do not make significant long-term behavioral changes in our youth. Only through the teaching and practicing of new and appropriate skills will we be able to successfully impact our youth. Active Learning gives you an avenue to present new skills and information in a manner that motivates students to become involved in their own learning process. Many lesson plans have a method for them to practice the skill and then to evaluate what took place. It is during this discussion time that much of the applied learning takes place.

"Researchers tell us that learning is more effective when increasing numbers of the five basic senses are involved", so states Edward Scannell in his book *Games Trainers Play*. The more senses that are involved, the better our retention of the information will be. This is based on connectors. When we are able to connect information with something tangible, it is easier to recall and apply. The more connectors we have, the easier it is to transfer the information to different areas of our lives. If we really understand something, then we can apply it to situations that are similar but not necessarily identical. This is the underlying goal of many of the skills that we teach our youth. It is through Active Learning that we can create many of these connectors. In his book *Do It! Active Learning In Youth Ministry*, Thom Schultz relates "Contrived experiences provide almost as much learning potential as direct, purposeful personal experience. These contrived activities can be performed in the classroom. Games, simulations, and role plays, when carefully planned and later debriefed, can result in real learning with lasting implications."

Seven Excuses for Not Using Active Learning

1. **Games are for kids.** Some teachers feel that their students are too old for activities that look a lot like playing games. They claim that their students are too sophisticated to be participating in such activities. In reality what you will find in many cases is that the teacher doesn't like to play games; it has nothing to do with his/her students. Active Learning has been successful in classrooms across the country. Rich kids, poor kids, urban kids, suburban kids, old kids and young kids alike have found that, when properly presented, games can be fun.

2. **I need to tell my students what is important.**
   This is the philosophy behind lecturing. The students need to have information poured into their brain from a source that is more knowledgeable. I agree that for some kinds of information this is appropriate, but it is taken too far by too many. According to the publication *Communication Briefing*, "forty percent will forget what you've said after twenty minutes. Sixty percent of the kids will forget after half a day and a full ninety percent will forget after a week." Active Learning allows the students to tell each other what they thought was important with the teacher guiding those findings.

3. **Not enough content.** It is true that during the Active Learning lesson there will be less information taught than during some other types of teaching methods. This is why you need to have a balanced approach to teaching and use a variety of methods. When you discuss content, remember that there is a difference between what is taught and what is learned. Just because the information has been presented, doesn't mean that it has been internalized. Ice cream is great, but too much of it and the appeal is lost. Too much information or content presented at one time has the same effect. Our brain can only absorb so much at one time and then it begins to selectively remember what is being said or in some cases just turns off altogether.

4. **Too noisy.** Have you ever walked by a classroom and heard a lot of noise and even laughter coming out of the door, so you stuck your head in and there was the entire class up out of their seats? I know some people that would automatically assume that

not only is learning not taking place, but that the teacher has lost control. We need to break out of the mold that quiet classrooms mean learning is taking place: Tell me how much noise day-dreaming makes. A room of thirty kids, all actively involved, produces noise. It also produces learning - more learning than a room of thirty kids sitting passively while the teacher drones on for extended periods of time.

5. **Takes too much time.** It depends on how you measure time. If you mean that an Active Learning lesson takes more time to complete than some other forms of teaching to get information to students, you are right. This teaching technique is not for large units of information that has to be given out quickly. It should be used when you want to affect a person's behavior, attitude, social skills or other life skills. The beauty of the technique is that once the teacher establishes the activity, the students teach themselves with guidance from the teacher. It may take longer than lecturing, but the outcome in terms of behavior change and retention is well worth it. The amount of time used is greater when your class is first experiencing Active Learning. Once the structure, format and process have been established, your class can move into the activity and the discussion in shorter and shorter time frames.

6. **Loss of control.** Teachers like to be in control of their students. Active Learning does not take away this control, but it does share that control with the students. This sharing takes place when the activity is underway. The teacher is there to monitor and be sure that the safety rules are followed, but basically stays in the background. However, even during

the discussion time when control looks to be with the students, the teacher can maintain control since he/she is the one asking and directing the questions. A positive aspect of giving away some control is you get to see what your students are thinking instead of what the teacher is thinking.

7. **Too set in your old ways.** It doesn't matter how long you have been teaching, you will have heard the phrase "It's always been done that way." We are comfortable with the familiar and therefore, look with disfavor on anything that might change what we are used to. New ideas need to be approached one small step at a time. Since the Active Learning technique is not an entirely new way of teaching or even a new curriculum, teachers can just get their feet wet and try out the water. Then as time goes by, and you feel more comfortable with the lesson plans, you can broaden your thinking and start adapting the lessons to better fit with your personality and the group of students you are teaching.

Chapter Five

Conducting an Active Learning Lesson

"In Active Learning, kids may learn lessons the teacher never envisioned. Because the leader trusts students to help create the learning experience, kids may venture into unforeseen discoveries. And often the teacher learns as much as the students."

Thom Schultz

Your enthusiasm for the activity will be the catalyst for the excitement of your students. If you approach the activity with an air of expectancy, this feeling will rub off on your students. Unfortunately the converse is also true: If you approach an activity with low key expectancy - so will your students. Active Learning, while being educational, is fun. Don't take the fun out of the experience by your attitude. Instead, let your attitude be part of the fun!

Tips on Leading an Activity

1. **Create a physically safe environment in which the activity can take place.** This can be dealt with by simply looking around the space you have

chosen to conduct the activity and checking for hazards. The hazards may be removed or pointed out so they can be avoided. If necessary, use spotters during the activity to be sure students don't run into objects or fall. Talk to the students about safety and remind them that activities can be dangerous if your directions are not followed correctly.

2. **Create a psychologically safe environment in which the activity can take place.** Psychological safety needs to be dealt with through the structure that you set up. There needs to be strict rules concerning put-downs, sarcasm, name calling, and other psyche-harming behaviors. Your tolerance towards allowing this kind of behavior will go a long way in setting the tone for the student's behavior during the activity.

3. **Establish a "freeze" command.** Work out some kind of signal word or noise, such as a whistle, that always means everyone needs to stop immediately. This signal can be used when a situation has become unsafe or if you wish to give further instructions. If you are close to a light switch, turning the lights off and on works really well. Just make sure that the students are not involved in anything physical, where a moment of darkness might cause a stumble or a fall.

4. **Remove students who refuse to cooperate.** If a student chooses to misbehave in such a manner as to make the activity unsafe, either physically or psychologically, they must be removed from the activity. You might want to set-up a warning system, such as one verbal warning before removing them, but do

not let the actions of a couple of people ruin the activity for the group as a whole. If the incident warrants such action, then immediate removal is certainly permissible. Allow them to rejoin the activity at the next logical break. Continue to monitor their behavior and discuss problems with them after the activity is over. Participation is a privilege, not a right and you should treat it as such. Be consistent in dealing with those that misbehave. The activities that are listed in the book are fun to do and most students will reconsider when they find themselves excluded.

5. **Directions should be short and to the point.** The longer you talk, the less they will listen. Remember that the central part of the lesson plan is the activity. You need to get them into the activity as quickly as possible. I find it best to give them directions after you have already formed them into whatever groups are needed for the particular activity. This breaks your directions into at least two sections. The first portion is how to form the groups needed, and the second is how to conduct the activity itself.

6. **If possible, demonstrate what you want them to do.** Modeling is always an excellent teaching tool. It helps them not only hear what they are to do, but see what they are to do. You don't have to show them step-by-step. This might defeat the purpose of the activity. You should only demonstrate difficult directions or those directions that would benefit most from a visual explanation.

7. **Be prepared for an imperfect first experience.**

If this is the first time your students have even been involved in Active Learning or something similar, they may not know how to respond. You will need to give much more guidance to your group the first few times they experience this type of learning. Many of them are used to being told exactly what to do and staying in their seats to do it. The less structured atmosphere of Active Learning may be difficult for them the first few times it is tried. Don't despair! This is normal and will pass. Keep trying; the rewards in increased student participation and retention of content are well worth the seeming chaos in the beginning activities.

The teacher's role in Active Learning

1. **Be personally enthusiastic.** No one else is going to be excited about the activity if you come across as bored with the whole thing.

2. **Maintain control over your students during the activity.** Keep a close watch on the students as they participate in the activity. This is not a time to correct papers, fix the bulletin board or any other housekeeping chores. Your full attention needs to be with the kids. It only takes a moment for an unsafe procedure to take place or a breakdown to occur in the safe environment.

3. **Be the time keeper.** Some activities will require time periods to be kept. The teacher should be the one that does this rather than assigning it to a student. Sometimes you need to adjust the time to better fit the ability of the group. Many times this does not become apparent until the activity is underway.

If you are the time keeper, you can make appropriate adjustments to better accommodate your students. Use your inner sense to know when to make the time shorter or longer to allow the activity to have more impact.

4. **Be flexible.** Too many times we think we know just how an activity should proceed, and when something different happens we panic. Active Learning has many different paths it can follow. As long as there is learning taking place, let the activity continue. Watch for unexpected teachable moments; they may come at any time during the activity.

5. **Watch, Watch, Watch!** Since each group has their own distinct personality, they will add something different to every activity. You need to be aware of the dynamics that are taking place: Who is doing what and how are their actions impacting the rest of the group? Your observations will form the thrust of the discussion that follows the activity. You may even want to write down some notes to help you remember significant actions or dialogue that took place during the activity which you can use during the discussion time to help the class process what took place.

Chapter Six

Choosing Partners and Dividing Into Groups

"Choosing teams embarrasses those who have the misfortune of being chosen last, especially if they're always chosen last or think they are."

Wayne Rice

In groups all over America, one of the toughest aspects of using active learning is having kids choose partners or break into groups. One difficulty lies in the fact you don't always have even numbers to form the pairs or groups that you need. An even greater difficulty might be that everyone in your group is not equally liked or that you have cliques that always want to be together. I do not see being with friends in some circumstances as a negative factor. However, if being with their friends becomes a problem or diminishes the effect of the activity, then it must be dealt with. Feeling left out when trying to find a partner or group is not a positive experience under any circumstances. Let's explore both of these troublesome areas.

Getting the Right Number of People

Not having the right number of people should not deter you from using an activity. When choosing partners, you as the leader have the option of being a participant or not. It is true that if you participate, you are not as free to watch others and see how they complete the activity. If this is not a crucial part of the process, then by all means participate. However, if you need to be free during the activity, the next best option is to pick three of your most mature kids and have them work together in a threesome. The advantage of selecting which kids will be the threesome is that you can choose individuals that will likely be able to finish the activity in a shorter period of time. By completing the activity ahead of the others they will then have time to have the other person in the threesome experience the activity while the rest of the group is still finishing.

What will usually not work is to have three kids who could not find a partner work together in a threesome. Many times these individuals take a little bit longer to finish than some of the others in the group and therefore they will not be able to complete two rounds while the rest of the group is completing one round. I do not say this because these individuals are not as smart as others in the group, but if they are not quick in choosing a partner then they may not jump right into the activity either. The slower speed with which they approach the activity might not allow them to complete two rounds while others are completing one round.

What if you are dividing into teams or groups of five and you only have twenty-three people? Here are a couple of suggestions.

If it is a relay activity, then simply have the teams with only four on it have one team member go twice. This way they will have five attempts just like the teams that have five on them.

If it is an activity where time or total points are the object, then you can make it the team's average score instead of the total score. For example, let's say that you are adding the scores of each individual team member together to make the total team score. Well if one team has five members and another team has only four, then the team with five would have an obvious advantage. To even out the scoring, total up the team score and then divide it by the number of people on the team. This will give you a per person score and will allow teams with different number of players to be comparable. I don't emphasize the competitive part of the activities, but the kids will want an equal opportunity at winning even if there isn't a prize. This method will allow the competition to be fair even if the teams are not evenly divided.

Choosing Partners

Choosing partners is sometimes a scary activity in itself. No one wants to be the last one to get a partner and how embarrassing it is if you end up without a partner at all. In some groups this is not a problem while in other groups this is a major concern. Here are a variety of methods I have used to help this process along. Since these methods take a little longer than just saying "grab a partner," you may want to keep the same partners for more than one day of activities. Before you even start doing activities, you will need to emphasize the feelings of others and that sounds of disgust, dismay or "put down language" will not be acceptable behavior. These techniques might take the burden from the teacher or leader as being the bad guy who assigns partners.

1. Have everyone form two circles, one inside the other. The two circles should have equal numbers in each. While you play music, sing a song, count out loud or whatever, have the two circles walk in opposite directions. When the music stops, the person opposite from you is your partner.

2. On a piece of paper put the names of half of the members in your group. Assign numbers to each one of these individuals. List these numbers on the board. Now have the other half of your group take turns picking a number from the board. Write their name next to the number they have chosen. When everyone is finished, reveal who the numbers on the board belong to. You have now picked partners without anyone even knowing who their choice was when they picked. Explain that there will be no changing of partners once they have been chosen.

3. Create two wheels out of two pieces of construction paper or tag board. One piece should be larger than the other. Connect the two pieces of paper by joining them in the middle with a single brad. This will allow the two pieces of paper to be rotated. Put the names of half your group on the outer or larger wheel and have the other half of the names on the inner or smaller wheel. When it is time to assign partners, simply turn the wheel and partners will be assigned automatically.

4. Put the names of everyone in your group on 3 X 5

cards. Put the cards in a hat or box and pull them out two at a time. The people that are pulled out together are partners.

5. Have your group line up in a single file line by birthday, height, shoe size, etc. Once they are in one long single file line, have the line fold in the middle. Whoever ends up opposite you when the lines fold is your partner.

Forming Groups or Teams

Forming teams or groups is not nearly as scary as choosing partners. When you say "form teams or groups of five" there is enough confusion that no one is really noticing how the groups are formed. However, sometimes it is preferable for you to help form the groups or teams. This is especially true when you are first beginning to use activities with your group, at the beginning of the year or when your group is new to each other. This just takes away one more thing for them to think about. Here are some procedures that I have used.

1. Nothing is easier than simply counting off by however many groups you want. If you want to jazz this up a little, try this. If you want five groups instead of having them count off up to five, make up a short sentence. For example, if you want five groups you could use "The eagle was really mad" as your sentence. Go around the room and have each person say one word of the sentence. The sentence would be repeated as many times as necessary to allow everyone in the room to say one of the words. When you are done, all of the same words would group

together. Everyone that said "the" would be on one team, all of the "eagles" would be on one team, etc. If you need more or less than five groups, then make your sentence longer or shorter. Be sure that you don't have any words in the sentence that would make people embarrassed. A sentence such as "The pig was really mad" might make those who were on the "pig" team not very happy. Also to avoid confusion, do not repeat any words in the sentence.

2. Have your group line up in a single file line using different criteria. Some examples of this would be: By length from your elbow to the end of your index finger (shortest to the longest), number of people in your family (fewest to the most), hair color (lightest to the darkest), etc. They will already be mixed up, so simply divide the group into the number of teams that you need. If you want teams of five, count off the first five and that is a team. Continue to do this until you have everyone on a team.

3. Divide your group by the number of letters in their last name. You can make the groups by a certain number of letters. They could be grouped with others who have five or less letters in their name. Those that have six to eight letters in their name. Those that have nine to twelve letters in their name. If the groups don't come out exactly as you need them, then divide the larger groups into even smaller groupings either by using their first name or by another grouping such as height. This method usually needs some fine tuning by the teacher or group leader since it doesn't always divide the group into exactly what you need.

4. If you need two teams or four teams, then here is a quick method that works well. Have the entire group count off from one to however many people there are in the group. Then have the odd numbers form one team and the even numbers form the other team. If you need four teams rather than two, then repeat this process one more time with each of the two teams numbering off separately and then once again splitting into odd and even.

One concern that many leaders have is splitting up friends. I have been on both sides of this philosophy. Yes, it is good for kids to meet and work with new people. This is part of the reason that we have interaction as part of these activities. If this is a key component of the activity, then by all means be sure to split your groups so friends are not together. If during whatever process you use to divide into groups you end up with pairings that you feel will not be beneficial to the learning environment, then simple move people around. The reason for using a device for grouping is to get away from awkward situations that might occur. But the dividing process should not take precedence over your knowledge and past experiences with the individuals in your group.

I do not feel that friends should always be divided. Let them experience working together during activities that do not call for exercises where familiarity will diminish the learning process. If you let them be together for some activities, it will not be as hard to keep them apart when it is necessary.

Chapter Seven

Discussion: The How and The Why

"Conversation is the laboratory and workshop of the student."

Ralph Waldo Emerson

There are many terms used to define what takes place after an activity. These terms include discussions, processing and debriefing. All mean essentially the same thing, which is to talk about what just happened and to determine its application to real life. Carmine Consalvo in her book *Workplay*, describes it this way, "Processing or debriefing refers to the questioning and discussion that follows the game. It strives to elicit critical reflection based on observations regarding what happened in terms of both external interactions and internal reactions."

The role of the teacher during the discussion is a critical one. The teacher needs to assume the role of guide rather than traffic cop unless something is said that will damage the discussion or is so blatantly incorrect that it needs clarification. If clarification is needed, see if asking the students for clarification is possible, rather than jumping in and stopping the flow of the discussion. More clarification and teacher involvement will be needed with younger students and even with older students when you are getting your class used to the discussion format. Skill must be used to steer the discussion rather than control it or dominate it. A good healthy discussion flows around the teacher not back and forth from teacher to student.

The teacher has basically two roles during the discussion. The first role is to establish the format by deciding how people will take turns talking and provide a safe environment for opinions. The second role is one of asking questions. This will consist of opening with a question that reviews the activity which just took place and then to continue asking questions that help the students explore the activity and apply it to their lives. If you wish a free exchange of ideas during the question time you must be sure that you do not interject your own opinion either overtly or covertly. If this occurs the students will start searching for the "right answers" based on what they think the teacher wants rather than listening for what each other thinks. Be careful of what you say after a student has had a turn. If you enthusiastically nod your head, say "great answer", or any other comment that can be interpreted as complimentary then you affirm that answer. Instead, adopt a standard set of remarks that show you heard the student, appreciate their comments and that they have finished making their remarks. A simple "thank you" or " OK" will accomplish this.

Do not be afraid of silence during a discussion. Too many times teachers ask a question and then, while their students are thinking, jump in with another question. Give them some time to collect their thoughts and formulate an answer. If you truly believe that you have asked a question that is too difficult to answer, then wait a short while and rephrase the same question so they won't have to start thinking all over again. Once the discussion has concluded, you should resume the role of the teacher and summarize what has been said and restate the important concepts that have been brought out.

A discussion emphasizes learning rather than teaching. Students are not only thinking about the issues, but they are also learning to ask the right questions of themselves and others. This is the beginning of critical thinking which is the basis for many of the skills needed to deal with the issues that will trouble them as they work towards adulthood and independence. Research has shown that information which is discussed, rather than just heard via a lecture, is remembered longer and becomes more meaningful to students. This is due to the fact that students are required to rephrase the information in their own language. When students share aloud, they become more confident in their opinions. This helps shape their thinking and eventually their behavior. It is better that their opinions are shared and shaped in the classroom where you have some control over the situation, rather than the streets where a voice of reason may not be present. Your presence has some impact on what is said and the direction of the discussion can be tempered by the questions you ask.

A discussion can reinforce opinions and values your students already have but were afraid to admit because they felt no one else felt the same way. This is a good exercise in positive peer pressure. A teacher can preach the evils of anti-social behavior and not reach kids, but if a classmate says the same thing the impact is greatly increased. A discussion can also help nurture communication skills. We know that good communication is the foundation for success in life. A good discussion can educate your students by its process as well as by what is said. The chance to share ideas and opinions creates the opportunity for kids to become better communicators - as speakers, listeners and thinkers.

Benefits of Having Discussions

1. **Students learn to take turns speaking.**

2. **Students learn to value each person's opinion and experiences.**

3. **Students can experiment with new thoughts opinions and ideas in a safe environment.**

4. **Students can develop the skills of observation, analysis and logic.**

5. **Students learn to clarify and review what they have learned.**

6. **Students will learn opinions that differ from their own and can expand their body of information to create new opinions.**

7. The teacher can evaluate a student's knowledge about and understanding of the information being discussed.

8. The teacher is able to hear what his/her students are thinking, feeling and experiencing in a non-threatening environment.

9. The teacher can have dialogue with a large number of people at one time.

10. Allows for structured exploration of a topic using comments that the participants think are important rather than just what the teacher feels is significant.

11. Is student oriented, yet teacher controlled.

12. Very flexible and adaptable to varying age groups, maturity levels and topics.

The Basics of Starting A Discussion

Ground rules for a great discussion

1. Personal issues which are brought up during the discussion time stay in the room and are not to be repeated to friends, family or others.

2. There will be absolutely no put downs, sarcasm or humor directed towards or at the expense of another person.

3. There is no such thing as a dumb question, comment or opinion. Everyone has the right to ask or say what they want as long as it is appropriately expressed.

4. Individuals can be encouraged to talk, but no one is forced to talk.

5. Out of respect for the speaker, only one person talks at a time.

6. Be sure that you have prepared your basic questions ahead of time.

7. Try to get as many people talking during the first few minutes of the discussion as possible.

8. Do not be afraid to let the discussion go off track as long as it is filling needs. The students may have a better idea of what is relevant to them than you do. Use another question to refocus the discussion rather than pointing out the fact that the discussion is off track.

9. If the class is in excessive agreement, play the devil's advocate to stimulate critical thinking.

10. Don't be afraid of silence.

The Magic of Questions

I cannot stress too strongly the importance of the discussion time following an activity. The activity is not complete without it. If you see that time is running out, cut down on the activity rather than eliminate or dilute the discussion. Questions are the focal point of a discussion. What you ask and how you ask it will greatly determine the success of the discussion and the concepts explored.

The first rule of any discussion is for you to determine which direction you want the discussion to go. This keeps significant issues from being lost when the discussion becomes side tracked. The question or comment a teachers uses to start the discussion is important because it sets the trend for the rest of the discussion. Good discussion questions will focus on a person's opinion, experience or feelings. There are no right or wrong answers for these types of questions. Good discussion-starting questions will begin with why, explain, how, what do you think, etc. This type of phrasing lets the students know that there is something to discuss rather than a specific answer being looked for.

Active Learning becomes a learning experience when we reflect upon what we have done, what impact that has and how to apply it to our lives. This can be summed up in three questions - What happened? So what? and What next?. To expand these questions just a bit, think of the three areas that they cover. The first set of questions reflect on the activity itself. What just happened here and how do you feel about it? The second area concerns what we can learn from the activity. The third is how we will be different because of what we have experienced. These areas can be explored with three types of questions. The first is "Launching Questions." These get the discussion going. Everyone participated in the activity so everyone can answer these questions. The second is "Understanding Questions." These will ask about feelings and concepts that were brought out during the activity. The last is "Applying

Questions." These will ask how the facts, concepts, and principles from the activity can be applied to their lives.

Questions to Avoid

1. **Questions that have a right or wrong answer.**

2. **Questions that can be answered "yes" or "no."**

3. **Long wordy questions where the meaning is forgotten before you even stop asking.**

4. **A question within a question.**

5. **Questions that are either - or.**

6. **Questions that have an obvious answer.**

7. **Questions that are too general or too vague.**

8. **Questions that the students do not have enough experience to answer.**

Questions That Can Be Used To Keep Your Discussion Going

Sometimes after you have thrown out your thought provoking opening question, the discussion starts to run into some rough spots. This is where your question asking skills will become important. You can use questions to help clarify statements, to look at an issue more deeply, to redirect the discussion to another student or to draw someone into the discussion.

"Can you give us example . . . "

"What did you mean when you said . . . "

"What makes you believe that?"

"Please explain what you just said."

"What reason do you have to feel that way?"

"What part of the activity do you base your opinion on?"

"Could you expand on that?"

"What other feelings did you feel?"

"Please tell us more about . . . "

"What did you mean by . . . ?"

"What else can you add?"

"Susan, what do you think about John's answer?"

"Jesse, tell us what you think."

"Well, we have heard from Mindy. Greg what do you think?"

"Thanks Armando. Jessica what do you think?"

"Brandon you have said a great deal. What do others think?"

When asking these questions, be sure that you do not give the impression that you are asking the individual to defend their answer. You are just seeking further information that would help the discussion.

Getting Kids to Talk

Some students will hesitate to speak in a group because they are shy or they feel that their contribution is not very valuable. They feel that the comments and opinions of others are more important than theirs. You can use a variety of techniques to draw them into the discussion that is taking place or future discussions. Realize that everyone benefits from a discussion, not just those that talk. Your students will learn just by listening to the questions and hearing the discussion that takes place.

1. **Start with questions that are non-threatening and not too personal.**

2. **Use questions that ask for opinions rather than facts.**

3. **Use an activity as a basis for the discussion so everyone has the same experience to draw from.**

4. **Have the students write down their opinions and then read them to the class for comment.**

5. **Ask for a comment from someone who has not contributed yet.**

6. **Ask a student what they thought of another student's comment.**

7. **After class talk to students who are habitually quiet. Ask them some questions and when they answer, explain that those are worthwhile opinions and you would like to have them expressed so everyone can benefit from them.**

Chapter Eight

Discussion Hints

"Effective communication involves the pleasant paradox of more listening than talking."

Karl Rohnke

During my workshops I receive a lot of questions about leading a discussion. This particular aspect of Active Learning seems to create a great deal of anxiety for those who are just learning to use this teaching strategy. In this chapter I have addressed a wide variety of these questions surrounding the issue of discussions.

"Help! I can't get my kids to talk during the discussion time."

Getting kids to talk has always been one of the toughest parts of leading a discussion. It results in a pretty short discussion when you are the only one talking. Here is a method I have started using that has been a great way to generate input from kids who normally say very little.

The technique works like this. Take pieces of tag board or 4 X 6 note cards and print feeling words on them with a magic marker. Only print one feeling word per card. Then after an activity has been completed, spread these cards on the floor or a table. Direct the students to look over the words and choose the card that most closely explains the feelings that they experienced during the activity. You might want to have duplicates of certain feelings if you think that many students might have shared that same feeling. However, don't let them get stuck on just one feeling. They will have experienced more than one feeling during the activity, so direct them to choose a card that is left which most closely describes a feeling they had. If you have a small enough group or there are a lot of feeling cards left after they all make their first choice, offer to let them make an additional selection.

Once they have chosen their cards, have the students sit down. When everyone has been seated, have them share their cards with the group. During the sharing have them explain why they chose that particular feeling card and what happened during the activity to make them feel that way. This can be done in a large group or you can break them into smaller groups to share. Remember that you want to have as many students discussing as possible. Smaller groups will allow this to happen. If you have broken into smaller groups, then as part of closure you may then have some people share again with the entire group.

I have found that by using the cards, kids are more willing to share. They use the card as a crutch that allows them to hide behind the paper like it is the paper talking rather than them. By choosing the card, they have already made their decision on what they want to talk about. When it is their turn to talk, they feel quite free about explaining why they chose the card rather than being stuck on explaining the feeling. I realize that choosing a feeling card as opposed to choosing a feeling out of their head may seem like a small difference to you, but believe me when I say it makes a real difference with your kids. This is an especially good tool when dealing with younger kids who have trouble verbalizing or older kids that don't discuss easily.

Here is a list of feeling words that you can start with. Add to this list words that are common with your kids. My own collection of feeling cards includes over one hundred words.

excited	silly	surprised
angry	bored	disappointed
determined	worried	sad
proud	lonely	scared
embarrassed	happy	frustrated
important	challenged	picked on
anxious	organized	overwhelmed
effective	powerful	infuriated
restless	confused	exhausted
intelligent	defeated	eager
pressured	ignored	terrible
mixed up	cheerful	relaxed
emotional	flexible	calm
stupid	helpless	disagreeable
hurt	bitter	nervous
irritated	tense	threatened
lazy	bossy	quarrelsome

"How do you determine what kinds of questions to ask?"

I usually divide the discussion questions into three categories. The first set of questions ask "What?" You want to know what went on during the activity that the participants found interesting and how they felt during the activity. The second group of questions center on "So what?" Now that you have discussed what happened, you want to process how this activity applies to us right now. You explore applications to the situations that your group is in at this stage of their lives. The third set of questions should move to "Now what?" Take the lessons learned in the activity and apply them to a change of behavior for the future. "How can this information affect you in the future?" "What changes in behavior can result from this information?"

By using this broad outline for your discussion, you can build as many questions into each of the three sections as you want. If the activity itself needs a lot of processing, you can spend more time there. If there is a problem within your group at the present time, then ask more questions about their present situation. If it is a change in future behavior that you are after, then expand upon the application section. Decide before you start the activity what your desired outcome will be and prepare questions that will move you toward that goal. However, remember to stay flexible enough to flow with the comments of your students. You want the discussion to address their needs as well as your own.

"What are some really good questions to ask?"

The one question that I use most regularly is this: "What can this activity teach us about . . . ?" Many times the activity itself has been so clear that the kids are ready to jump right in with what they think. I still use the lead up questions talking about the activity itself, but when I get ready to switch over to using the activity as a teaching tool, this question is the one that I most often use. It is especially effective if your group has been doing these kinds of activities for a while. They will be used to tying the activity to some kind of lesson. One of my regular weekly groups of high risk kids are already saying, "I know what you are trying to teach us" before we even finish the activity in many cases.

Another good thing about this question is that it helps me see where the group is. I let a number of people respond to this question and then I can pick from those responses which direction or directions I feel we should go in processing the activity. Many times, if something has been bothering the kids, they will relate the activity in some way to what is the hot topic for them. This allows me to tailor the discussion around their needs while still reaching my desired objectives with the activity and the discussion. Give this question a try and see how it works with your kids. Realize, though, that it should be reserved for a group that is experienced in group discussion. If you use it with an inexperienced group, you will probably be met with uncomfortable silence due to their still trying to give you the "right" answers.

"Should I have a set list of questions that I want to ask during the discussion time?"

You don't have to stick to a set list of questions, but you do need to have a general sense of where you want the discussion to go. Here is a list of general suggestions that might help you in leading your discussions.

1. **Decide where you want to end up.** Don't be like the archery person who when asked how he always hits the bull's eye replied, "Oh it's simple. I shoot first and then draw the circle around where I hit." When you start an activity you should have some idea of how you want it to be processed. The discussion may not always go the way you want it to, but at least you will know when it strays or when you have reached your objective.

2. **Many roads lead to the same place.** If you want to travel across town you can take a number of different roads to get there. Don't restrict your group discussion to the one road you had decided to take. Keep asking questions until you arrive where you want. You can use questions to get you back on the right road if the group has strayed too far off the topic.

3. **Get as many people involved as possible.** The teacher standing in front of the group asking questions is not always the best discussion format. Use partners, small groups, written comments, small group reporting out to the large group, etc. The more kids that are talking, the more involvement and learning that is taking place.

"How long should I spend discussing?"

This is a tough question to answer since so much of it depends on the activity that you have conducted, the topic that you are discussing, the amount of previous knowledge regarding the topic, the age and mental development of your group, past experience your group has had with processing and the time your schedule permits.

Let's take a look at these factors. Some activities have a lot of directions that you can go and others are trying to get a single point across. If it is a single point activity, don't try to make the discussion time last forever. Let a few questions solidify the point and move on. I am afraid that some people determine the success of a discussion by how long it lasts. The longer the discussion, the more successful. Not true! Some of the activities are so clear in what they show that the point is immediately obvious. The same is true with certain topics. If it is a cut-and-dried fact about a certain drug or behavior that you are trying to impress upon your kids, then discuss long enough to make the point and move on. However, many times the topics are such that they can be applied to many different issues. In these cases, decide which ones would be most applicable to your group and cover as many as the group can handle.

Previous knowledge, either that the group brings to the activity or that you explored with them before conducting the activity, has an impact on the processing time. If the students are very familiar with the topic, then more discussion will be generated. If it is a new idea or concept to them, then you will have to take it in shorter time segments and address the topic with multiple activities or lesson plans over a longer period of time. Also, consider the developmental stages of your kids. During different developmental stages they are ready for different approaches to the same concept. As they mature mentally, they will be able to discuss for longer periods of time and, more importantly, with more complexity.

Past experience or familiarity with the processing process also plays a part. The more experienced your group becomes in sharing opinions and ideas with each other, the longer and more in-depth the discussion time will be. You will have to be patient with them during this learning period.

They will be testing you to see if you are acknowledging "right" and "wrong" answers. Do not do this. If you reply after each comment, then you will be giving away your feelings as to what they are saying. Comments such as "Excellent," "Good," "I like that," etc. can reveal which answers you support and which ones you do not. A better method is to just acknowledge each answer with "Thank you" or "OK." They will also be testing the psychological safety of the classroom climate to see if they are ridiculed or teased for comments they make. The facilitator plays a major role in making the discussion time a safe one for kids to share their thoughts.

The last item is the time you have allocated for processing. If you have scheduled twenty minutes and it only lasts ten, then you need to be sure that you have something else to fill the remaining ten minutes rather than trying to fish for more discussion. Conversely, if you have scheduled twenty minutes and your time is running out, then you need to be sure that the important parts of the activity are addressed.

I feel that time should not be the deciding factor in determining the length of a discussion. Interest that is generated during the discussion should be your guide. If the kids are still volunteering information, then you should keep the discussion going. Some of your most meaningful discoveries will be made after all of the obvious answers have been given. Conversely if you are pulling teeth to get participation, then you need to either end the discussion or change the line of questions to something that is more relevant and appropriate for your group.

The real answer to the question, "How long?" is let your group tell you. If their participation isn't meeting the needs of your lesson plan, then go back and reconsider how you are asking your questions and how you are structuring the discussion process.

"What can I do to end a discussion?"

Sometimes when a discussion is slowing down, you would like to do something that adds closure to the activity. One good technique is to have each person complete a sentence. You can have everyone complete the same sentence stem or you can have a variety of stems for them to choose from. The only rule is that they can not complete the sentence with a phrase that has already been used. Each person must have an original contribution or be ready to explain how their statement is different if someone else has already said almost the same thing.

Here are some of the sentence stems that I have used:

In today's activity I learned . . .

In today's activity I relearned . . .

In today's activity I was surprised . . .

In today's activity I was pleased that . . .

One thing I have learned from this activity is . . .

I can use what I learned from this activity when I . . .

One thing that I will share with my parents from this activity is . . .

If you would like to follow-up, simply ask for an explanation or reason for their choice of answers. This is a great activity to do in groups of about five people. They can share their answers with the others in their group. If time permits, you can randomly select individuals or call for volunteers to share their answers with the entire group after they have shared in their small group.

One additional question that I have used to be sure that everyone is finished with the discussion is a simple but effective one. I conclude with, "Are there any last thoughts before we move on?" This question gives the group a chance to express any unsaid comments.

Chapter Nine

Discussion Formats

"Processing or debriefing refers to the questioning and discussion that follows the game. It strives to elicit critical reflection based on observations regarding what happened in terms of both external interactions and internal reactions."

Carmine M. Consalvo

Many factors play a role in having a good discussion; Such simple things as the set-up of the room can impact the success of your discussion. If you want to generate discussion among your students, the best seating arrangement is one that allows all of the students to see each other. It does not take very long for your students to rearrange themselves into a circle or a square. After practicing a couple of times, most classes can reduce the time and noise associated with this change to a minimum.

Where the teacher stands is another factor. If the group is in rows facing the teacher, then the teacher is the focal point of all of the comments. If the students are seated in a circle and the teacher stands at one end, the teacher will still command the discussion. If you want the discussion to be as student oriented as possible, then the teacher should sit in the circle with the students. Many teachers start their class off with the teacher being the dominant person in the discussion. Then as the class becomes more comfortable with the discussion format, the teacher moves off of center stage and allows the discussion to become more student centered. The timing of such a move will depend upon the age, maturity and ability level of your students.

There are many different formats that can be used for discussions other than the traditional "teacher ask - student answer" format. A few of these are listed in this chapter. Once again, I urge you to use your own creativity to adapt these formats or create one of your own for use in your classroom. I would recommend that you vary the format of your discussions, as students enjoy change in their learning environment.

Large Group: This is basically the traditional format where the teacher asks the questions and the students respond. This is the easiest format to use in the beginning because the students are already familiar with it. This format also allows you the most control over the discussion and the class.

Small Groups: Divide your class into groups of about four to six students. Have them spread out around the room and discuss the activity. You can give them one question and have them discuss it until you call time and then give them a second question, or you can put all of the questions on the board or on a hand out for them to answer in their groups. If you want the class to stay together and work on the same question at the same time, you could put the questions on an overhead transparency and reveal each question as you feel the class is ready to move on. For accountability, you can randomly ask one or two groups to share with the rest of the class the main issues discussed in their groups.

Buzz Groups: Divide your class into groups of between four to six students. Have each group select a leader and a recorder. The leader is responsible for keeping the group on task and the recorder writes down the group's ideas. You can use the same steps as found in the "Small Group" format for asking the questions and keeping the groups together. When you have covered all of your questions, have the recorder or a designated spokesperson from each group share their comments. After that, you may want to open up each question for large group discussion or follow-up with additional questions for the large group or the buzz groups.

Partners: The more students that you can involve in the discussion time, the more learning takes place. Have your students pair up with a partner. Once again you can give them a list of questions, have questions on the board and reveal them one at a time, or ask questions one at a time for them to discuss between themselves. Randomly ask pairs to share what they discussed. You could then follow-up with additional questions for the entire group or for them to discuss further with their partner.

Written Answers: Some students do not react well to the pressure of a discussion. They need private time to collect their thoughts and form their answers. Have your class answer the basic questions that you would like to ask in writing before you open up the discussion.

Let them keep the paper in front of them and read the answers they have written when called upon. For some reason, students seem to feel more comfortable reading an answer. This works especially well with groups who are just learning how to discuss.

Written Comments: Again, have your students write down their answers to your questions. Then collect the papers and read some of the answers to your first question. Ask students to comment on what you have read. Then go onto the second question and repeat the process. This allows you to hear from students who would not normally respond during the discussion time. It also disassociates the comment from the person. Comments can be read and discussed while the contributor remains anonymous. This is a good method to try if your class is reluctant to share their opinions in a group setting.

Agree - Disagree Continuum: This format requires your students to physically commit themselves to a point of view. In your room, assign one wall of the class as the "Strongly Agree" side and the other wall as the "Strongly Disagree" side. Read a statement and tell your students to line up between the walls according to how much they agree or disagree with the statement that you just read. They can arrange themselves from one side of the room to the other, with those in the middle having opinions that both agree and disagree with the statement you read. Once they have arranged themselves, ask various students to explain why they chose to stand where they did. Start with one side of the room, then go to the other and finish with those in the middle. Ask at the end if anyone would like to reconsider where they chose to stand and ask them to explain why. Then read a second statement and have them once again choose where to stand.

This is an excellent way to have the entire class participate, even if they all don't get a chance to explain why they chose their particular spot to stand. Simply by having to move from one spot to another, they had to think about the question. It is also a good activity to talk about peer pressure and what impact where friends chose to stand had on students. The most difficult part of this format for the teacher is writing a good statement. It must be controversial enough so some students will agree and others will disagree. Remember that you do not use questions, but rather statements.

Thumbs Up: A less time consuming variation to the above format works with a signal to designate how much you agree or disagree with a statement. One good signal makes use of the thumb. You read the statement and then the class agrees by giving the "thumbs-up" sign, disagrees by giving the "thumbs-down" sign and is in the middle by pointing the thumb sideways. You may call on them to explain their particular choice. This format does not have the same impact as lining up because students can hide their signals or not commit.

Videotape: As an aid for getting a discussion going, videotape the activity the students were involved in. Show the video tape to the class and stop it at strategic points. Ask the class what they saw going on and discuss various segments.

Tokens: This format helps when you have a few students who dominate the discussions. Give everyone a certain number of tokens or chips. Each time they have a turn during the discussion, they must surrender one of their tokens. When they are out of tokens, they can not say anything else. You may give out more tokens as often you like.

Flying Ball: If your class is having trouble with the concept of only one person speaking at a time, this is a fun format. Get a small nerf ball or similar object that has enough weight to it to be thrown, but not enough weight to hurt people. The only person that may talk is the one that has the object. It is thrown from speaker to speaker and physically shows who has the floor at the time. This is especially good with younger classes.

Chapter Ten

Using the Active Learning Lesson Plans

"You can lead a horse to water, but you can't make him drink. Wrong! You can feed him salt."

Howard G. Hendricks

These lesson plans were written for individuals, such as teachers and others who work with young people, who might not have a lot of experience in leading an Active Learning lesson. Those who are experienced in this or similar teaching techniques, will find the following explanations very basic. Those who find this teaching technique as a new or unfamiliar challenge will discover more use for these instructions. I would encourage all teachers to use these lesson plans as only a starting point for your own creativity.

Topic Area: A listing of the topics for which discussion questions have been developed. If more than one topic is listed, there is a comma between the topics. You should rarely try to address more than one topic, unless it is alcohol and other drugs, during a single lesson. Use your own judgment about how many topics your students can handle during one activity and discussion time. There are many more topics that can be addressed for each of these lesson plans than I have indicated. In many cases, topic application is limited only by your own imagination and ingenuity.

Concept: An explanation of why this activity is important and how it can be applied to your students. This section will give you a basis for information that should be presented before the activity. Remember that activities should not stand alone. Introductory material needs to be given to help in understanding and applying the concept that is experienced during the activity. Without a strong introduction and solid follow-up, an activity becomes just fun rather than a learning opportunity. However, don't go too far when introducing the activity. You want this to be a discovery process; let the students experience and then discuss the activity. Major concepts will be more significant if they are discovered during and after the activity by the students rather than by having you explain the important concepts or key points to them.

Method: Only two classifications are used. One is Classroom demonstration. Here the teacher undertakes an activity in front of the class. One or more students may be involved in the demonstration. The second method is Classroom activity. Under this format the entire class will be directly involved in the activity. The teacher's role will be to facilitate the activity and be sure a safe environment, both physically and psychologically, is provided. Consideration should be taken as to how much room will be needed for a particular activity. You may have to rearrange chairs and tables in your room or even move to a larger facility, which could be indoors or outdoors.

Time Needed: This is only an estimate based on the past history of these activities. Your class may take longer or shorter. Some consideration might need to be given to how quickly your group understands directions and can set-up for the activity. Extra time can be consumed when teams are chosen, room arrangements made or materials distributed. Once your group gets accustomed to the Active Learning format, they will become more adept at the logistics of getting ready. Remember you need to allow time for introductory material and follow-up discussion time. This time has not been figured into the time needed estimate.

Materials Needed: Each activity has been designed with as few materials needed as possible. If handouts are called for, they will be found at the end of the activity. You can photocopy as many classroom sets for your own use as you need. Most materials are easily found and cost very little. Extras should be on hand in case they are needed during the activity. I would hate to see an activity fall apart just because a prop is misplaced or broken.

Activity: This is a description of how to conduct the activity. Instructions are given on how to set up the format of the activity. I would suggest that you go through the steps of each activity before you try to conduct it with your group. Sometimes things that sound easy when you read them, suddenly become confusing when you try to put them into practice. If you get in the middle of an activity and find something not working correctly, stop and give further instructions to make changes which will work. Be sure that you can explain the activity clearly and easily. It is best if you can demonstrate movements that might be difficult before you ask your students to try them.

If teams are called for, the numbers I have given are flexible. Decide what would work best for your group. If you have an odd number that will not make even teams, you can have one or more people go more than once to even things out. If it is a partners activity then you might choose to participate.

If you would like to spice up your activities and make the kids think they are really hot stuff, here is a suggestion for you. Increase the amount of points that you give for scoring purposes. Instead of giving one point for each correct answer, give 100 or even a 1,000 points. The scores add up real quick and make the activity take on a whole new atmosphere. Who wants to end a game with ten points when they could have 10,000. It is also a sneaky was to get some different math skills into your activities.

Some of the activities have scenarios and stories in them. When you use them, please change the names of the characters to fit the ethnicity, culture and diversity of your area. Since my activities are used all over the country, it is impossible for me to choose names and describe situations to match each local area. I have tried to be as generic as possible so the activities can be used in a number of geographic areas. Use your own judgment to make these activities reach the diverse populations that you serve.

Don't try to do too many activities in one day. For these to be most effective, each one should be given full attention. If you do too many, one right after the other, the students start to look at them as games rather than learning activities. The discussion time is the key. If you take the proper time to discuss each activity, then the opportunity for life changing learning will present itself.

Variations: Not many of these have been included. Your willingness to think and be creative is the only thing holding you back from making dozens of variations from these listed activities. I encourage you to send any variations or new activity ideas to me to be included in future publications and workshops. Some of the ideas in this book were given to me by innovative teachers. Let me help you share your creativity with others.

Discussion Ideas: Just a few questions to help you get started. These questions will help you follow-up with the topics listed at the start of the lesson plan. The discussion time is absolutely necessary to complete the activity. Spend some time before you conduct the activity to think about the questions you would like to ask and in what order you would like to ask them. Watch your students during the activity and questions will pop into your mind. Try to keep most of your questions open ended with no right or wrong answers. The questions that I have listed are in only a general order. They are not meant to be used first to last. Use these questions as a jumping off point and then use others to explore important issues that came up during the activity or during the discussion.

Appropriate Age Levels: You will notice that this category has been left off of the lesson plans. The reason for this omission is simple. I could give suggested grade levels, but then you might not read a lesson that could easily be adapted to your grade by simply changing one aspect of the activity. Another reason for not suggesting grade levels is some classes are very advanced and some are not. By not predetermining what grade level each lesson plan fits, you can make your own decision based on what you know about your class rather than what I think about a lesson. So go ahead and read them all. Use what works and change what doesn't.

Active Learning In Action: How about a real life example from someone in the field. Judith Schmid wrote to tell me about her experience with one of my activities. The activity is called "A Cents of Floating". You will find it later in the book. Judith works at the Salt Lake County Youth Services Center in the Interim Shelter Program. Here is her letter.

Seven p.m. is a restless time in the Interim Shelter at the Salt Lake County Youth Services Center, a 24 hour crisis intervention center for runaway and ungovernable youth. The client population was typically diverse—five females, ranging in age from 12-16, and 7 males, ages 11-16. The ethnicity of the group included Caucasians, Hispanics and Polynesians.

For group time that night I placed straws, a basin of water, masking tape and pennies on the table. After pairing the kids up, I explained the goal of the activity. "That's dumb" and "Why do we have to do this?" were among a few of the responses I received. "Just give it a shot and see what you can do," I replied.

One team set to work immediately. Another pair was "fencing" with straws, while others debated where to begin. Minutes passed and I reminded them of the time factor. That got their attention. Exchanges between partners became focused and intense. I finally called out "Time! Let's see what you've done."

The first team took their turn. Their raft floated until 13 pennies weighed it down and water seeped into the ends of the straws. After two more teams, the group decided it wasn't fair to move the basin in front of each team because it created "high waves" so the basin stayed put.

After all the teams finished, they asked "Can we try again?" After processing the successes and shortcomings of each raft we began round two. Materials were handed out, the clock was started and the teams began. This time the teams got about building right away. Each team was focused and intent on their "task".

Again the groups gathered around the basin of water. One team shouted, "We want to go first and we're gonna win!" As each penny was placed on the raft, the entire group began to count out loud. High fives and groans were exchanged among partners. Four of the six pairs were able to place more pennies on their rafts during the second round, while one team matched their previous effort and one team floated less.

During the discussion time we talked about group efforts, contrasted their first attempts with their second, and asked what they would do differently if they were given a third opportunity to try again (which many of them wanted to do). I asked, "How is this like real life?" Kids talked about baby-sitting jobs, deciding what to do on a Friday night and about playing on a soccer team. I asked, "What have we discovered about working with others?" One answer was, "Sometimes it's easier than other times, depending on who you're working with and what you have to do." Several members of the group concluded that "trying what works for other people may also work for me."

Thanks Judith! Well, there you have it. A real life description of one group's experience. More happened than Judith could share in the letter, but it does give you some idea of the group dynamics involved in Active Learning. Your group's first experience could be better or it could be worse, but give it a try and above all else, remember to have fun!

***Check the back of the book for information on bringing Tom Jackson to your area to teach a half-day or full-day workshop where you can have hands-on experience in conducting Active Learning lesson plans.

Chapter Eleven

Active Learning Lesson Plans

"Learning can take place at three levels - cognitive, affective or psychomotor. The acquisition of knowledge, attitudes or skills can be expedited through the selective utilization of an appropriate game."

Edward E. Scannell

"Yes, you can learn about a football game by watching it on television. But you'll learn more and remember the game longer if you join the team and play."

Thom Schultz

A CENTS OF FLOATING

TOPIC AREA: Problem Solving

CONCEPT: Critical thinking and decision making are areas in which our youth need practical experience. The ability to visualize a problem and to create a solution are not innate abilities within most of our students. Working with a partner to verbalize ideas and make decisions regarding problems are skills that must be developed in our youth. This activity gives them a tangible outcome to work with and a challenge to explore.

METHOD: Classroom activity

TIME NEEDED: 30 minutes and discussion time

MATERIALS NEEDED:

- 10 drinking straws for each team of two (Your local fast food establishments will more than likely donate these to you)
- 50 inches of masking tape for each team
- 1 or 2 pans with about one inch of water in them. I use the disposable baking pans that you can find at the grocery store.
- 100 pennies

ACTIVITY: Have each student in your group pair up with a partner. Give each team 10 drinking straws and 25 inches of masking tape. Explain that they will have seven minutes to design and build a raft. They may only use the straws and masking tape that they were given. The object is to build the raft so that it will hold the most pennies before sinking. When they are finished, they are to bring the raft up to the pan of water for their "official float."

Have the teams build their rafts. Do not let them try to see how well they float before the official float. They may use the entire seven minutes you have given them or they may come up and do the official float before the seven minutes are up. For the official float, they will put their raft in the pan of water. Then the team members themselves will take pennies and place them *one at a time* on the raft. They may put the pennies anywhere on the raft that they want to. They will keep adding pennies, one at a time, until the raft goes under water. The total number of pennies on the raft before it sank is their official total.

Now give them a second try. They will have to use the same ten straws, but you can give them a new 25 inches of masking tape. All of the rules stay the same for the second try.

VARIATION: Sometimes I let the teams use scissors and other times I don't. It doesn't really seem to make a lot of difference in the design of the rafts nor in the activity itself. It does give them one more thing to think about. You can make the decision yourself. Most of the fast food places are using plastic drinking straws. I can tell you from experience that they are real hard to cut without scissors. If you have access to a bunch of scissors without a lot of work getting them, then it makes the activity just a little more complex.

DISCUSSION IDEAS:

- How many pennies did you float on your first try? Your second try?
- What kind of design ideas did you have?
- Was it hard for you and your partner to agree on the design?
- Did you stick with your original design concept? If not, what changes did you make?
- Was your original design idea the best one possible or did you make improvements as you went along?
- Did you watch other teams to see what they were doing? If you looked, did you get any good ideas from them?
- Is it permissible to watch others and get good ideas or should all of your ideas just come from you and your partner?
- Is getting ideas from others called "cheating?"
- What changes did you make when you tried making your second raft? Did they help?
- Did one of the two of you dominate the building or was it a shared experience? Explain.
- What frustrations did you have during the activity?
- If you had it to do over again, what changes would you make, either in the design or placing the pennies?
- What does the word "compromise" have to do with this activity?
- How can we apply this activity to real life?
- How does this activity apply to the workplace?
- Would you like a job where you have to make decisions or would you like to be told what to do? Why?

A GOOD BUY

TOPIC AREA: Friendship

CONCEPT: Friendship is a highly sought after relationship. The good feeling that comes from having friends can help in avoiding some of the problems associated with the teen years. Acceptance has been pointed to as one of the reasons for joining a gang. Acceptance has also been noted as an underlying cause for peer pressure being as powerful as it is. If having friends is so important, then we need to spend some time on the skills associated with being a friend.

METHOD: Classroom activity

TIME NEEDED: 30 minutes and discussion time

MATERIALS NEEDED:
* None

ACTIVITY: Divide your group into teams of three to four people. Explain that they are to write a newspaper, radio or TV advertisement to sell a friend. The advertisement can be just words, it can be a rap, song, jingle or poem or it can even be a short skit that they act out. The key is that it must be advertising the characteristics of a friend. They can not tell about the looks or body features of the friend. You can set a minimum of how long the advertisement must be or just leave it up to them. If you wish, you may allow them to use any props that they can find in the room. Give them about fifteen to twenty minutes to create the ads and then have each group share their advertisement with the rest of the group.

VARIATION: You can turn the assignment around and offer the option of looking for a friend instead of selling one. The concept is the same. They still advertise for the characteristics they want in a friend rather than the physical attributes.

DISCUSSION IDEAS:
- How hard was it for you to create the advertisement?
- Could your group agree which qualities of a friend should be in your advertisement?
- What qualities were expressed by more than one group?
- How easy is it to find all of these qualities in the same person? Why?
- Which qualities are the most important ones to have in a friend?
- Are people born with these qualities or can you become a better friend over time?
- What does the saying "To have a friend you must be a friend" mean?
- Why is it so hard for new kids in school to find friends right away?
- What are some ways to make friends?

ADD A WORD

TOPIC AREAS: Diversity, Working Together

CONCEPT: When there is a problem to solve or a discussion about a topic, the more people that provide input the better the outcome. People bring a wide variety of experiences to any given situation. These experiences can help to see things in a different light or to provide a different viewpoint. If everyone works alone with only their own experiences to draw upon, then they have a very narrow reservoir of knowledge to draw upon. Even if they work with others who have had the same kinds of experiences and background that they have, the pool of knowledge is still somewhat limited.

METHOD: Classroom activity

TIME NEEDED: 15 minutes and discussion time

MATERIALS NEEDED:
* One piece of paper and a pen or pencil for each team of four
* A watch with a second hand

ACTIVITY: Divide your group into teams of four. Give each team a piece of paper and a pencil or a pen. Explain that the object of this activity is for each team to create the longest sentence that they can. You will give them the first few words to the sentence. Each person will then take turns adding one word at a time to the sentence. The sentence must make sense and it must come to a logical ending. The paper and pencil must be passed from person to person as they add their word. They may not talk at all during this part of the activity. They will have sixty seconds to complete their sentence. Call out the time so they will know how long they still have to write.

After you have called time, have each group count up the number of words that they used including the words that you gave them to start with. Have them write this number to the side of their sentence. Have each group tell how many words they used. Ask for volunteers to read their sentence aloud. Repeat this process three or four times. Here are some of the sentence starters that I have used.

The cow jumped . . .

A worm crawled . . .

A loud crash . . .

People who are . . .

The next time . . .

A woman screamed . . .

One dark night . . .

After you have completed three or four rounds, change the rules. This time the paper and pencil must still be passed from one person to another and each person may still only add one word at a time, but the group may talk among themselves to make suggestions on what the sentence will say. Once again only give them sixty seconds to create their sentence. Call out the elapsed time for them to hear. When time has ended, have them read their sentence aloud and tell how many words they used. Repeat this twice. You should notice an increase in the number of words that they were able to write when you compare the very first try where they couldn't talk with the very last try where they could talk.

DISCUSSION IDEAS:
- How well did your team do when you couldn't talk?
- How easy was it to figure out which word to use next?
- How much pressure did you feel when it was your turn? Explain.
- How did the activity change for you when the group could talk?
- Was your team able to create longer sentences when they could talk? Why or why not?
- How much pressure did you feel when the group could make suggestions? Explain.
- When you have a problem to solve how much help is it to have someone else give you suggestions?
- Will a greater number of people always make it easier to solve a problem? Why or why not?
- How can people with different backgrounds than yours help you solve a problem?
- Why would it be important for people of different backgrounds to work together on problem solving?
- What could someone from a different culture provide that you couldn't?
- How can different viewpoints help solve problems?

ANIMALS "R" US

TOPIC AREA: Self-Esteem

CONCEPT: Each of us is unique. This uniqueness sets us apart from everyone else. If we were all the same, we would lose many of the contributions that make our society special. Each person has some qualities that are special just to that person. A particular quality may be found in abundance in some or it may be found in a small dose. It doesn't matter how much of each quality we have or don't have, because each and every quality is not in every person. It is the mix of qualities that we find in the individual and how they use those qualities that makes that individual unique, special and a valuable member of our community.

METHOD: Classroom activity

TIME NEEDED: 25 minutes and discussion time

MATERIALS NEEDED:
- Paper and pencil or pen for each team of three
- A watch with a second hand

ACTIVITY: Divide your group into teams of three. Give each team one piece of paper and a pen or pencil. Explain that you will write the name of a person on the board. Choose a name with some vowels, no duplicate letters and around five letters. For example, you could use the name Sharon or Brent. Each team is to write the name in large letters across the top of the paper. Leave room between each letter. Draw lines between each of the letters in the name. Have the lines extend down from the name so that you have created columns for the teams to write in.

When the activity begins, you will give each team six to eight minutes to list as many animals as they can think of that begin with each letter that is in the name. They are to write the animal names in the columns on their paper under the corresponding letter from the name that you gave them. Explain that they will be scored two ways. The first scoring will be the total number of animals that they have listed. They will then receive bonus points for each animal they have listed that no other team has listed. Knowing this they will want to balance out quantity with creativity.

When time is up for them to write down the animal names, you will score the results. Have them count up the total number of animals that they have listed. Put this figure at the top of the paper. Now have each team read their list of animal names aloud. Have each team go through one column completely before going on to the next column. Have the first team read their list under the first letter. If another team has the animal listed that the leader read, then they need to raise their hands. All teams that have that animal listed will scratch that name from their list. Each team will read their animals and everyone will cross out any animal mentioned by another team. The only names that score bonus points are the ones that no other team has on their list. These animal names are worth two points each.

Continue this scoring for each column. When all of the columns have been read, the teams will total up all of the animal names they had listed that no other team read out. Remember that these are worth two points each. Add these points to the points they received for each animal they listed and this is their total score. Repeat this activity twice using two different names.

DISCUSSION IDEAS:
- How hard was it to think up the animal names?
- How well did your team do in thinking up names that other teams had not thought of also?
- Did your team go for quantity or creativity with their names? How well did your strategy work?
- Were some letters easier than others? Which ones?
- Was the second round any easier than the first? Why or why not?
- What were some of the unique animals that were listed?
- Are all animals of one species the same? In the way they look? In the way they act?
- How is a cat different than a hamster?
- What do we do differently with a dog as opposed to a horse?
- Does the differences in animals make them good or bad? Explain.
- What abilities do some animals have that other animals don't have?
- How about people? What kinds of things make them different from one another?
- In what ways do people look different from one another?
- In what ways do people act differently from one another?
- In what ways do people have different abilities and characteristics?
- What are some of the abilities or characteristics that

some people have that other people don't have?
- Why do you think we have so many different kinds of people?
- Do the differences in people make them good or bad? Why or why not?
- How are individual people unique?
- How does this uniqueness make our society better?
- What would happen if we were all the same?
- We don't see horses trying to be birds? Why do we see some people trying to be things they aren't?
- How should we feel about the qualities and characteristics that we each have?
- What should we do if we aren't satisfied with things that can be changed about ourselves?

ATTENTION

TOPIC AREAS: Drugs, Gangs

CONCEPT: Both drug usage and gang membership sneak up on you without you realizing how much control they begin to have over your life. The early drug user and the gang wanna-be believe that they are in control of their lives and many times even use the cry of freedom to justify their participation in these activities. However, as they become more deeply involved their lives begin to be controlled by the activity rather than their lives controlling the activity. The use of drugs or gang activities begin to take over and are the focal point of their daily existence. At this point personal freedom is lost as their focus of attention and their choices are determined by events outside of their control.

METHOD: Classroom activity

TIME NEEDED: 25 minutes and discussion time

MATERIALS NEEDED:
- 1 large shirt with buttons for each team of five people
- 1 hat for each team
- 1 balloon, plus some extras, (9 - 11 inches, the larger the balloon the easier) for each team
- Masking tape
- A watch with a second hand

ACTIVITY: Place a piece of masking tape on the floor at one end of the room to designate the starting line.

Divide your group into teams of five. Have each team line up behind the starting line in a single file line facing you. About fifteen feet in front of each team place a shirt and hat. To be fair you should have the same number of buttons on each team's shirt.

Explain to the team that this is a speed relay. The object is for each team member to run down to the clothes and put them on and take them off. Once they have done this they are to return to their team and the next person in line goes up and does the same. The game ends after each person has had one turn. Be sure everyone has had a turn before you end the activity. They must completely button the shirt up when they put it on and unbutton it to take it off. Record the completion time for each team.

For round two add a blown up and tied off balloon to the clothes pile of each team. Before they may start putting on the clothes, they must hit the balloon in the air. The balloon must remain in the air the entire time each person is putting on and taking off the clothes. If the balloon hits the ground then they must take off the clothes and start again. The balloon does not have to be in the air while they are taking off the clothes to try again, but it does have to go back in the air once they start over again. The balloon does not have to stay in the air while the team members are switching places. Record the completion time and compare with the first round.

DISCUSSION IDEAS:
* How well did you do when it was your turn to change clothes?
* What problems did you have when changing clothes?

- How did the activity change when you had to keep the balloon in the air?
- How hard was it to keep the balloon in the air when you changed clothes?
- Where was your attention focused when the balloon was added to the activity? Why?
- How could this activity relate to the use of drugs?
- How do drugs take your attention away from what you are doing?
- How much control do drugs have over your life once you start using them?
- How could this activity relate to gang membership?
- How does a gang take your attention away from what you are doing?
- How much control does a gang have over your life once you join?
- How easy is it to succeed in the other parts of your life (school, work, sports, hobbies) when you have to keep your attention focused elsewhere?
- How would this situation affect your life?
- Is this a positive or negative situation? Explain.
- Do you feel personal freedom is important? Why or why not?
- How do drugs or gangs take away your personal freedom?

BALANCING ACT

TOPIC AREA: Being Flexible

CONCEPT: As we go through life sometimes we need to be flexible. If we are too rigid about what we want or the direction our life is going then we cause problems for ourselves. Setting goals and having "To Do" lists are fine as long as they don't create undue stress in our lives or make us unpleasant to be around. The key is to be flexible. Be willing to make small changes and compromises that do not effect your life in a major way, but do allow others to get along with you.

METHOD: Classroom method

TIME NEEDED: 20 minutes and discussion time

MATERIALS NEEDED:
- 6 one half to one inch in diameter and three foot long wooden dowels

ACTIVITY: This activity will involve having kids see how long they can balance a wooden dowel upright on their hand. They must put their hand out flat and balance the dowel in the palm of their hand. Give each person in the group a chance to practice with the dowels before you start the competition.

Begin by selecting six people to be in the opening round. Let them all get their dowels balanced and then say go. Have the people who are not in the contest at the moment help judge. They need to watch and be sure that no one starts to cup their hand to make it easier. When someone's dowel either hits their body or falls on the ground, they are out. Continue this round until you have two or three people left in that round. Keep going until everyone has had a chance to compete.

Once everyone has had a chance, start the next level of competition. This level will be for those who survived the first round without dropping their dowel. Once again have them go until there are a couple of people left in each round. Eliminate enough people that for the championship round you will only have as many people as you have wooden dowels.

Then have the championship series. This is a head-to-head competition among those that are left. If balancing seems to be too easy, add the new rule that they can't move their feet. Another way to make it harder is to have them close one eye while trying to balance the dowel.

DISCUSSION IDEAS:
- How hard was it to keep the dowel balanced?
- What methods did you use to keep it balanced?
- How easy would it be to just stand in one spot and keep it balanced?
- How hard would it be to never move your hand and keep it balanced?
- In your daily life do you have to keep juggling things around to keep everything going?
- How hard is it to keep up with all of the demands on your time and energy?
- If you were very rigid in the way you did things, would your life be easy?
- How does the word "flexible" fit into your life?

- How would you treat a person who had to always be right?
- How would you treat a person who had to have everything their way all the time?
- What part does compromise play in our daily lives?
- If we refuse to compromise how will others treat us?
- Should we compromise on all issues? Which issues should we not compromise on?

BALL TOSS

TOPIC AREA: Goal Setting

CONCEPT: When setting goals, you don't want them to be too difficult or too easy. If they are too easy then the challenge of accomplishment is lost and if too hard, then discouragement becomes a factor. Other aspects of goal setting that need to be addressed include having others help you reach your goals and the reason for setting a goal in the first place.

METHOD: Classroom activity

TIME NEEDED: 20 minutes and discussion time

MATERIALS NEEDED:
- 3 tennis balls for each team of 4 - 6
- 1 bucket or trash can for each team
- 1 blindfold for each team
- A pencil and piece of paper for each team

ACTIVITY: Divide your group into teams of four to six people. Each team will need a pencil and a piece of paper on which to keep their score. Give each team one tennis ball. Put a bucket about 10 feet in front of each team. The person who is going to throw must either be blindfolded or have their back to the bucket. Have each person on the team try to throw the ball in the bucket without looking. You can score this part of the activity in the following manner: give them one point if the ball hits the bucket, three points if the ball goes in the bucket and then bounces out and five points if the ball goes in the bucket and stays in. If you really want to make this part difficult, you can spin them around a couple of times before they get to throw the ball. This first part of the activity should be done separately from the rest of the activity. It is best done as a lead into why we need to set goals. You will need to process the fact that if you don't have any goals, then you won't know which direction you are heading or how to get there. Blindly throwing the tennis ball shows how hard it is to hit a goal you can't see or haven't set.

To start the rest of the activity, move each team's bucket about 35 to 40 feet in front of each team. Give each team three tennis balls. Have one member of each team go out and stand by the bucket. Each team member gets to throw three tennis balls at the bucket. The person's job by the bucket is to return the balls for the next person. Rotate positions so everyone gets a chance to throw. Have the teams keep a running score of how many balls go into the bucket. They get one point if the ball goes in the bucket and then bounces out and three points if it goes in and stays in. For the second round, move the buckets in closer to about 20 feet. Repeat the same procedure as before. For the third round, move the buckets in closer to 3 feet and repeat the process once again.

For the fourth round, move the buckets back out to the 20 foot mark. This time have one team member pick up the bucket and help get the tennis ball to land in the bucket by trying to catch it in the bucket. They may move only after the person throwing the ball has released it in the air. The procedure should be the same as previously used. Now check the team scores and see which team has the most points.

Hints for processing: The first step where they throw without being able to see the bucket helps show them that it is hard to reach a goal if you don't have one. In the first round when they have to throw the balls so far, you are showing goals which are too difficult hardly ever get reached. The second round is usually the best experience for them. In the third round, the bucket is too close for it to be much of a challenge. During the last round when you have a team member help by moving the bucket around, you are showing that it is easier to accomplish a goal when someone helps you.

DISCUSSION IDEAS:
- How did it feel when you were trying to get it in the bucket without seeing it?
- How can the blindfolded throw be compared to not having any goals?
- Are goals important? Why or why not?
- How did you feel when you were trying to hit the bucket at 35-40 feet?
- How did you feel when you were trying to hit the bucket at 20 feet?
- How did you feel when you were trying to hit the bucket at 3 feet?
- How was it different when someone was moving the bucket to help you make it in?
- How did you feel when you were the person moving the bucket?
- Should you set goals that are really difficult to reach? Explain.
- What are some examples of goals that are difficult to reach?
- Should you set goals that are easy to reach? Explain.
- What are some examples of goals that are easy to reach?

- What are some ways that people can help you reach your goals?
- What happens when other people set goals for you to accomplish rather than you setting your own goals?
- How can drugs, gangs, sexual activity or other self destructive behavior hurt your chances of reaching your goals?

BALLOON BASH

TOPIC AREA: Stress

CONCEPT: The stress in the lives of our young people seems to be growing by leaps and bounds. Many of the surveys that are taken of today's youth rate the area of stress as one that needs to be addressed. Alcohol and other drugs seem to be one of the favored outlets for those experiencing stress. Interestingly enough, even the use of tobacco has been rated as a stress reducer by kids. The use of these drugs actually creates more stress in their lives in ways that they don't even seem to recognize. Stress management techniques need to be taught as a viable alternative to the seemingly easy and foolproof use of alcohol and other drugs.

METHOD: Classroom activity

TIME NEEDED: 15 minutes and discussion time

MATERIALS NEEDED:
- 1 eleven inch round balloon per person plus some extras
- Masking tape
- 1 magic marker per team of five
- A watch with a second hand

ACTIVITY: Divide your group into teams of about five. Have the teams line up facing each other like they were playing the game "Red Rover". Put a piece of masking tape on the floor between each team to divide them from one another. The teams should stand about three feet back from the masking tape line. Give the person in the middle of each line a balloon. Have them blow it up as large as they can and tie it off.

Explain that the object of the game is a lot like volleyball without a net. Each team scores a point when a balloon touches the ground on the opposing teams side of the masking tape. There are no out of bounds, so the balloons may be hit over the teams heads. The balloons may only be hit using your hands. No kicking allowed.

Before that action begins, have each team use a magic marker to write one thing that causes them stress on their balloon. Have them be specific. Have each team share the thing that causes them stress aloud.

Play begins with the person in the middle of each line hitting the balloon. Each round is played for fifteen to twenty seconds. The teams may score as many points during the fifteen to twenty seconds as possible. When a balloon hits the floor, a point is scored by the opposing team and the balloon is put back into play by whichever player is closest on the side where the balloon hit the floor. Each team keeps their own score.

When time is over in the first round, check the scores from each of the teams. Before starting the next round and each successive round, have the players rotate positions. Have each team rotate in opposite directions so the players will not always be across from the same people.

For round two, have each team add a another balloon. There will now be four balloons in play instead of two. Before you start, have them write something that causes them stress on the balloons they are adding. Once again, share the stress items. Start the time again and play round number two. When time is over, check the scores. Keep playing rounds and adding balloons until there are almost as many balloons in play as there are people. Play will really be hectic by the time all those balloons are being used. At the end of each round, stop and check the scores.

DISCUSSION IDEAS:
- How easy was the activity when there were only two balloons in play?
- How easy was the activity when there were four balloons in play?
- What happened to the activity as balloons kept being added?
- What were some of the stressors that your team wrote on the balloons?
- How easy is it to handle one or two of these stressors in your life at one time?
- What happens when you have a lot of stress all at once in your life?
- What are some major situations that can completely stress you out all by themselves?
- What are some of the ways to reduce minor stress?
- What are some of the ways to reduce stress when it gets really bad?
- Can other people help you with stress? How?
- Why is using alcohol and drugs not a good method to reduce stress?
- What stress can alcohol and drugs cause you?

BALLOON JUGGLE

TOPIC AREAS: Drugs, Stress

CONCEPT: There are many facets to each of our lives. We have responsibilities in many areas. We have to balance school, chores, jobs, friends, family, church, hobbies, music lessons, sports and other interests into twenty-four hour days. When we attempt to take on too many responsibilities, our lives seem to resemble a runaway train hurdling down the tracks. We can't seem to get a handle on which thing to do next. Across the country I have been seeing more and more high school students carrying around day planners to help them keep track of their various meetings and activities. Something is wrong with this picture! As a society we honor those who take on a lot of responsibility and still seem to get everything done. When a child's life becomes this involved, they need to take a step back and look at what is important and what is not. Stress is not easy for anyone to handle, but definitely not someone who is still trying to discover what direction they want their lives to go. Is it any wonder that the teen suicide rate is increasing at an alarming rate?

If we add drugs to this picture, then it just increases the problem. No longer can students juggle all of their responsibilities because they are concentrating on their drug use. The drug takes over their life and causes them to neglect other areas such as school, family and work. This neglect leads to more stress due to undesirable consequences and many times the answer is simply increased drug use to relieve the increased stress.

METHOD: Classroom activity

TIME NEEDED: 20 minutes and discussion time

MATERIALS NEEDED:
- 2-4 round balloons plus some extras (about 9 inches in diameter) for each participant
- 1 larger round balloon for each team of 3 to 5 members
- 2 magic markers for each team

ACTIVITY: Divide your group into teams of three to five people. Give each team a magic marker, two to three balloons per person and one large balloon. Have them blow up all of the balloons, and tie them closed. Have each student use a magic marker to write activities that they are involved in on the smaller balloons (for example sports, music, etc.). They may put more than one activity on each balloon. On the large balloon have them write either the word "drugs" or list a number of individual drugs such as cocaine, cigarettes, beer, etc.

Once these props have been created, explain that the object will be for the teams to hit the balloons with their hands and keep them in the air for as long as they can. The team works together to keep the balloons in the air. If a balloon hits the ground then they must pick it up and start it again. Have each team start with one balloon per person. After a period of time, such as thirty seconds, have them stop and add a second balloon for each person. Have them keep track of how many times a balloon hits the ground during the thirty seconds. If you are dealing with an older group or one that can easily handle two balloons per person, then add a third and then a fourth balloon per person.

After they have experienced this, then have them add the balloon marked "drugs". Explain that they must keep the drug balloon in the air at all costs, even if one of the other balloons starts to hit the floor. No one may hit the balloon marked "drugs" two times in a row. At least two other people must hit the drug balloon before the same person may hit it again.

DISCUSSION IDEAS:

- What kinds of activities did you write on your balloons?
- Are some of these activities more important to you than others? Why or why not?
- Are some of these activities more important to your parents or other adults than to you?
- Why or why not? Which ones?
- How hard was it for your team to keep one balloon per person in the air?
- How hard was it for your team to keep two, three or four balloons per person in the air?
- How hard was it to keep the balloon marked with drugs in the air?
- What did you have to do differently to make sure the drug balloon did not hit the floor?
- How can we compare our own lives to keeping the activity balloons in the air?
- How do we know when we are "too busy"?
- Have any of your friends become so busy that they did not have time to just "kick back"? Explain.
- How can we compare the addition of the drug balloon to drug use?
- What effect do drugs have on a person's other activities?
- How can the use of drugs cause stress in a person's life?
- How can others help a person who is using drugs?

BANKROLL

TOPIC AREA: Values

CONCEPT: How rich you are depends on the perspective you are looking from. How much money is a lot of money? How do we define rich? These questions are answered differently by each and everyone one of us. A recent survey I read in the newspaper asked people "How much money would it take to make you feel rich?" No matter how much money people had, it was always more. Those making $30,000 thought it would be $100,000 and those making $100,000 thought it would be $300,000. The result of the survey was that everyone thinks they would be rich if they had more money. Very few people felt that what they had was enough. Do we place such a high value on money and material goods that we disregard the things that we already have? Does this desire for more money drive us to work harder, cut corners, cheat people and lie to get ahead? What values are we placing on money, material goods and the desire to have more and what role do these values play in determining our behavior?

METHOD: Classroom activity

TIME NEEDED: 10 minutes and discussion time

MATERIALS NEEDED:
• A pencil or pen and piece of paper for each person

ACTIVITY: Have each person in the group make a list of the clothes, personal care products and jewelry they are wearing. If they have braces on their teeth, have them include them also. If it is a younger group that is not wearing a variety of these items, then have them also include a list of the items from their bedroom such as toys, tapes, radio, video games, etc. The object is to have them come up with a list of items that are ordinary and accepted as common place for them to have, own or use.

Now have them place a dollar figure next to each item as to how much that item cost to purchase. Estimates are OK If they have included everyday items like deodorant or perfume, have them list the price of the entire bottle. After they have finished putting a price on each item, have them total up the cost of their list. Collect the papers and put the dollar amounts on the board. Do not identify which paper or total belongs to which person.

After completing writing the dollar amounts on the board, put the figure of $100-$300 on the board. Explain that this is the yearly income of many families in the countries of Africa and other parts of the world. With this amount of money they must buy food, shelter and the other necessities for their entire family.

DISCUSSION IDEAS:
* How does your list compare with the income of these families?
* How would you survive if that was all the money your family had to spend in a year?
* What would be the first things you would be willing to give up to reduce your figure?
* What would be the last things you would be willing to give up to reduce your figure?

- How important is money in our society today?
- Is this importance helpful or harmful to society? Explain.
- How important are the things we buy?
- How important is it for you to have the latest fad in clothes or trinkets?
- What kinds of things does the need for more money make people do?
- Does having money answer all of the problems that people have? Explain.
- What kinds of things can money not buy?
- Are people who have money more important than people who don't? Explain.
- Are people who have money treated differently than people who don't? Explain

BLANKET DROP

TOPIC AREAS: Self-Esteem, Stereotyping

CONCEPT: A person's name is an important part of their character. When we call someone by their name, it shows that we know them and are at least familiar with them. Having people call you by name creates a feeling of importance rather than hearing someone address you as "Hey you." However, just knowing someone's name does not mean that we know much about them. We should not judge others by just knowing a few facts about them. Before we make a judgment about someone, we should get to know them. If not, we might be stereotyping or generalizing rather than making decisions about them based on their own characteristics and qualities.

METHOD: Classroom activity

TIME NEEDED: 20 minutes and discussion time

MATERIALS NEEDED:
* 1 opaque blanket for each group of about sixteen

ACTIVITY: Any size group can participate in this activity, but if you get many more than sixteen, too many people are not participating. If your group is larger than sixteen, have more than one game going on at a time. All you will need is an additional blanket for each game.

The activity is started by dividing your group into an even number of teams, with about eight people on each team. Have two people stand and hold the blanket between them. The teams should be positioned on either side of the blanket in such a way that they can not see each other. Have them sit on the floor about five or six feet back from the blanket. Explain that they will choose a person to move up and sit down right next to the blanket, facing toward the other team. Both teams will do this. Once they are in position, the blanket holders will count to three and then drop the blanket to the floor. When the blanket drops, the two players who have been chosen to sit next to the blanket try to call out the first name of the person on the other side of the blanket before that person can call out their first name. The person who calls the name first gets a point for their team.

This process is repeated over and over again with different people being sent up to the blanket each time to face off with a person from the other team. A couple of rules: the people at the blanket may not disguise themselves or cover their faces; the members of the team who are not at the blanket may not shout out any information; the judges are the people holding the blanket. I would rotate these two people periodically with others on the teams.

VARIATION: Have two people from each team come up to the blanket at the same time. Have them sit side-by-side. The contest is still just between the two people sitting across from each other, but adding another pair at the same time creates more confusion and adds to the fun. In this case two points would be awarded for each round, with the fastest, correct answers receiving a point. You could also have them try to guess the person who is diagonally across from them instead of directly across from them. The judging becomes a lot harder under this format.

DISCUSSION IDEAS:
- How hard was it to say the name correctly?
- What made it hard to say the name?
- Was it easier to know the name when you were not the person sitting at the blanket, but just watching? Why or why not?
- Why is it important for you to know someone's name?
- How do you feel when someone calls you by name?
- How much do you know about a person by their name?
- Are all people named Tom the same? Explain.
- Is knowing someone's name enough to know very much about that person? Explain.
- What kinds of things should we know about a person before we can say that we really know them?
- How long does it take to get to know a person? Explain.

BLOW UP

TOPIC AREAS: Anger Management, Violence

CONCEPT: We need to know what makes us mad and when we are reaching our boiling point. Anger turns to violence when we allow our anger to control our actions. Anger itself is not a bad emotion, but the actions that come as a result of that anger can be negative. We need to look at pro-social ways that we can be angry and methods that can be used to reduce our anger.

METHOD: Classroom demonstration

TIME NEEDED: 10 minutes and discussion time

MATERIALS NEEDED:
- 2 large balloons, plus a couple of extras
- 1 sewing needle (the bigger the better)

ACTIVITY: This activity is done a little differently because you will stop in the middle of it and have part of your discussion. The second part of the demonstration will then take place and you will then discuss that portion.

Take a large balloon and blow it up part way. Explain to the group that the balloon is going to represent how angry we get. Ask for comments from the group as to things that make them angry. For each comment, blow the balloon up a little larger. At the same time, have someone write down on the blackboard the things that make people angry. You can control how many items get written on the board by how much you blow the balloon up each time something is listed. You will blow the balloon up until it explodes. If you can't blow it up large enough to pop it, have a needle or small pin hidden in your hand to make it pop at the right time. The object is to make it look like it exploded due to all of the things that make people angry.

DISCUSSION IDEAS:
- Why did the balloon pop?
- Do all of the items we listed on the board make us equally as mad? Why or why not?
- Does everyone react the same way to the items on the board? Why or why not?
- Do we react the same way to the same events every-day? Why or why not?
- How does the way we feel at a particular time affect the way we react?
- Can anger be positive? Why or why not?
- What are some of the ways that anger can be expressed so that there are not negative conse-quences?
- When does anger turn into violence?
- Why is anger OK, but violence is not?

Now blow up a second balloon. Blow it very large, but do not let it pop. Ask the group to give ways that we can reduce our anger. Have these listed on the board also. Let a little air out of the balloon for each technique they give you for getting rid of their anger. Once again, you can control the number of responses by how much air you let out of the balloon.

Do not let all of the air out of the balloon. Reduce it's size by about half. Tie the stem of the balloon. Now take a needle and tell the group that you will stick a needle in the balloon without popping it. To accomplish this, you will need to find the extra strong spot that is located opposite the stem of the balloon. This area is usually darker in color. Since the balloon is not blown up to it's full capacity, there is extra material at this point that creates a strong spot. It is directly into this strong spot that you stick the needle. Explain how you did this to the group. Show the extra material that is there because the balloon is not blown up all the way.

DISCUSSION IDEAS:
- Why didn't the balloon pop?
- Why is it important for us to know ways to reduce our anger?
- What are some positive ways we can reduce our anger?
- What are some negative ways we can reduce our anger?
- Do the same methods work for everyone? Why or why not?
- Do the same methods work for every situation? Why or why not?
- How can others help us reduce our anger?
- What role does anger play in violence?

BODY BASKETBALL

TOPIC AREA: Problem Solving

CONCEPT: Many times we work on problems alone and then become frustrated when the solution seems to elude us. Sometimes it is pride that makes us go it alone, other times it is stubbornness and in some situations it is just that we don't know who to go to for help. Being able to ask for help and knowing who to ask for it from are key ingredients in solving some of the problems that we face.

METHOD: Classroom activity

TIME NEEDED: 15 minutes and discussion time

MATERIALS NEEDED:
- 1 nine inch round balloon per person, plus a few extras
- 2 chairs
- String or rope about 15 feet long
- 1 to 3 trash cans or paper grocery sacks
- Masking tape

ACTIVITY: Set up the activity in an area that has about 15 to 20 feet of space in one direction. Set two chairs at one end of the room however far apart your string or rope is long. Stretch your rope from one chair to the other and tie it to the chairs. The rope should be about three feet off of the ground. Leave some space behind the rope at the end away from the starting line. Use your masking tape to mark a starting line at the end of the room opposite the rope. Put two or more (depending on how large your group is) trash cans or paper grocery sacks on the floor about two feet behind the rope.

Give each person a balloon. Have them blow it up as large as they can and tie it off. Explain that the object of the activity is to move the balloon from one end of the room to the other. They may not use their hands, arms or mouth to move or toss their balloon. When they reach the rope, they must get the balloon over the rope and into the trash can or bag. If their balloon touches the ground along the way or if they try to get it into the trash can and miss, then they must go back to the starting line and begin again. Allow the group about five or so minutes to try and accomplish this task. Do not give any suggestions on how to move the balloon. You will be amazed at the various techniques that will be used.

For round number two the rules are the same except that they will complete the activity with a partner. Even though they will each have a balloon, only one balloon will be used. The second balloon can be used if the first one pops.

DISCUSSION IDEAS:
- What methods did you try when moving the balloon by yourself?
- How well did these methods work?
- What methods did you try when moving the balloon with a partner?
- How well did these methods work?
- What did you find most difficult about the activity? Why?
- Was the activity easier or harder with a partner? Explain

- When trying to solve a problem, do you think that it is easier to do it by yourself or to get help from others? Explain.
- Are some problems easier to solve by yourself rather than with others? Explain.
- What are some problems that usually require the help of others to solve?
- What kinds of people would you seek out to help you when you have a problem?
- Have you ever been in a situation where you have provided help to someone else? Describe the situation.
- What are some of the reasons that people do not seek help even when they need it?

BOUNCE BACK

TOPIC AREA: Self-Esteem

CONCEPT: Bouncing back from problems is one reason we feel healthy self-esteem is such a vital part of a person's character. It is the difference between feeling things are your fault or the feeling that outside forces have created a problem for you, but you can handle it. When we feel there is no way for us to successfully handle a situation due to a low impression of our own abilities, then we find ourselves less likely to risk moving out of our comfort zone to attempt new things. If this pattern repeats itself over and over again, we soon find ourselves unwilling to try anything new and staying right were we are while others around us are moving ahead.

METHOD: Classroom demonstration

TIME NEEDED: 10 minutes and discussion time

MATERIALS NEEDED:
• One inflatable beach ball

ACTIVITY: Have the beach ball inflated before you begin the demonstration. Begin your presentation by explaining that you are using the beach ball to represent a person's self- esteem. Show the group how resilient the ball is. You can push in one side and it will pop back to its original shape. You can drop it on the floor and it will bounce back up.

Now ask the class to list things that might happen

during a normal day to kids their age which would lower a person's self-esteem. Tell them you are going to let some air out of the beach ball every time they name an event or situation that would lower their self- esteem. Don't let too much air out for each item. You want to stop when about one third to one half of the air has been let out.

Now once again push the side of the beach ball in and let them see if the ball returns to its original shape. Then drop the ball and point out that it did not bounce. After the discussion time, blow the beach ball back up and show that we can raise our self-esteem. Refer to the discussion question about ways to raise self-esteem and repeat what they said as you blow the beach ball back up a little at a time. Bounce the beach ball as a final reinforcer to what you have been talking about.

DISCUSSION IDEAS:
- What happened to the ball when I pushed on it when it had lots of air in it?
- What happened to the ball when I dropped it when it had lots of air in it?
- What happened to the ball when I pushed on it when it had less air in it?
- What happened to the ball when I dropped it when it had less air in it?
- What are some things which lower our self-esteem?
- Who are the people around us that affect our self-esteem? Why do they?
- Is low self-esteem a permanent thing? Why or why not?
- Is our self-esteem the same throughout the day? Explain.
- How can we raise our self-esteem?
- Who can help us raise our self-esteem?
- How can we help others raise their self-esteem?

BRAIN OVERLOAD

TOPIC AREA: Drugs

CONCEPT: Certain drugs have a stimulating effect on the brain. Two such drugs are LSD and Methamphetamines. Under normal circumstances, impulses in the brain travel along nerve fibers in orderly sequences. Serotonin, a neurochemical, permits impulses to jump across synapses from the end brushes of one sensory neuron to the dendrites of another. LSD and Methamphetamines interfere with the proper transmission of these signals, which results in distorted information being passed along. This can be compared to the spark plugs in your car firing off in powerful but erratic bursts, causing your engine to go haywire. These confused signals cause the brain to "see" music and "hear" colors. The individual may experience a feeling of floating outside their body or itching underneath their skin. They may also become depressed, restless, delusional, paranoid and easily driven to anger. When the brain becomes over stimulated, you lose the ability to concentrate on important information and find your thinking controlled by the drug instead of by you.

METHOD: Classroom activity

TIME NEEDED: 20 minutes and discussion time

MATERIALS NEEDED:
- One balloon for each person, plus a few extras (Use balloons of varying colors)
- Forty feet of rope or heavy string

- Whistle
- 5 chairs

ACTIVITY: Set the activity up as if you were playing four square. The rope represents the four square lines. However, instead of the lines being on the floor, place chairs at each of the four ends and one in the middle of the four square design. Tying the rope to the chairs allows it to be about two feet off of the ground.

Divide your group into four equal teams. Explain that the object of this activity is to keep the balloon out of your square by hitting the balloon over the rope, counterclockwise into the next square using only their open hand. If a balloon hits the floor before the whistle has blown, a player may pick the balloon up and slap it into the next square. You may have the participants stand, kneel or sit on the ground during this activity. The lower the position, the more difficult the activity. However, have everyone do the same thing. Do not have some people standing, while others are sitting. After each round have the participants rotate positions within their own square so everyone gets an opportunity to hit lots of balloons.

Begin by dropping or hitting one balloon into the game area. The kids will continue to hit the balloon into the next square until you blow the whistle. When the whistle blows, there is no more hitting . The balloon will be allowed to settle into whatever square it chooses. The team that has the balloon land in its square is given a point. The low score wins in this game. Repeat this activity a few times. Each round should last about fifteen to twenty seconds.

Now make it more interesting. Add three more balloons. Let each team start with a balloon in their square. The same rules apply as before except that one color balloon (of your choosing) is worth more points than any other color. The teams will want to be sure that this color is kept out of their square. After trying this a couple of times, keep adding balloons each round until you have more balloons than people. The first few rounds the kids will be able to keep the balloons moving from square to square without too many problems. As you add balloons, the action will become hot and heavy. You will have now created a situation that is very similar to what takes place in the brain when drugs have caused it to become over stimulated.

VARIATION: Have them change directions when hitting the balloons. This can be done before the hitting starts or when you blow the whistle in the middle of a round. If you use the whistle to indicate a change of directions, then use two short whistles to indicate that the round is over and hitting is to stop. Another option is to let them hit the balloons in any direction during the round. This really causes some great action.

DISCUSSION IDEAS:
- How did you feel when there was only one balloon in the game?
- How did you feel when there were very few balloons in the game?
- How did the game change as more balloons were added?
- How well did your team handle this activity?
- Did your team make any changes in their actions as more balloons were added?
- What impact did the special color balloon have on your actions?

- As more balloons were added, did the special colored balloon get lost in the action? Explain. How can this activity be compared to the use of drugs?
- How could the use of this type of drug affect your performance in school?
- How could this type of drug activity cause problems in your life outside of the classroom?
- How could this type of drug use affect your relationships with others?
- Would a person who used this type of drug lead a normal life? Explain.
- How would this affect you at the workplace?

BULL FIGHTS

TOPIC AREA: Gangs

CONCEPT: Protection is one of the reasons that we hear kids join gangs. Gangs give kids a group they can hang around with and that can provide help when they need to deal with other people. This sense of belonging and comfort is very important during the teen years. We know that gangs fill a real need in our youth. If a need wasn't being met, then gangs would not exist. We need to find ways that these same feelings and needs can be met outside of gang involvement and in a more positive manner.

METHOD: Classroom activity

TIME NEEDED: 15 minutes and discussion time

MATERIALS NEEDED:
- 3 spring type clothespins per person
- A watch with a second hand on it

ACTIVITY: Give each person three spring type clothespins. Explain that the object of the activity is to try to clip your clothespins on the backs of the other players. Each player tries to avoid being pinned. Pins may only be clipped above the waist and below the neck. You may not grab and hold players. Give them a time limit of about three minutes. You can adjust the time to fit your group while they are playing. Set some boundaries so they won't be running all over the place. The area of play should not be too large. You do not want them to spend all of their time chasing each other around instead of placing their pins on the backs of each other. At the end of this first round compare how many pins are on each person's back.

For round two, have them divide into teams of three people. Explain that the object is the same. They still want to place as many pins on the backs of others as they can. They want as few pins as possible to be placed on the backs of their own team. This means that they will want to work out a plan that will protect each other. Round two is played the same way as far as time limit and boundaries go. Once again, at the end of the time compare to see how many pins are on the backs of the various players. Have the teams stand together so you can see how they did protecting each other from enemy pins.

DISCUSSION IDEAS:
- How did you do during the first round of play?
- Was it hard to protect yourself from others when everyone was after everyone else?
- How did you feel when everyone was chasing you?
- How hard was it to place your pins on the back of other players?
- How did you do during the second round of play?
- How was the second round different from the first?
- Was it harder or easier to keep pins off of your back when you were part of a team?
- How did the team concept make the game different? Explain.
- How can you compare this activity to gangs?
- Do gangs provide protection from others?
- Are all gangs bad? Why or why not?
- For what reasons other than protection do people join gangs?

- How can protection and other needs be met without joining a gang?
- What are the benefits of being involved with an organized group such as a club, an activity group like Scouts or a sports team?

BY YOURSELF

TOPIC AREA: Suicide

CONCEPT: Some things are best done by ourselves. But there are times when we need the support of others to get through a problem we are facing or a situation we are in. This support network needs to be formed before we have a problem. If we have not cultivated people around us that we can turn to in a time of need, then by the time we have found someone to help us it might be too late.

METHOD: Classroom demonstration

TIME NEEDED: 5 minutes and discussion time

MATERIALS NEEDED:
• Four whistles or other noise makers that you blow

ACTIVITY: Bring one person to the front of the room. Give them one of the noisemakers and ask them to make an even and continuous sound in the background while you explain something. Tell them to start and then you begin to talk. It doesn't matter what you talk about. You just need to keep talking longer than they can keep blowing. Eventually they will falter. When they do, explain to them again that you need to have them hold a steady and continuous sound while you are talking. Have them try it again. Go through this same charade about three times. Then invite three more people up and give each of them a noisemaker. Ask the group of four if they can think of any way that between the four of them they could keep an even sound while you talk. If they can't think of a solution, open the question up to the entire class. The solution to the problem is that each one starts to whistle before the other one runs out of air. By having all four of them work together, they can keep the sound going on an even note for as long as they need to. Be sure you have them demonstrate this.

DISCUSSION IDEAS:

- What happened when just one person was trying to keep the sound going?
- What happened when other people helped the first person out?
- How can this demonstration be applied to our lives?
- What situations can we get ourselves into where we need the help of others?
- Have you had any friends that found themselves in a situation like this? Explain.
- Who are the kinds of people that we can turn to when we need help?
- What kinds of things can people do to help us?
- Is it a sign of weakness when we ask others to help us with a problem?
- Have you ever been able to help a friend when they needed it? Explain.
- Have you ever been helped by someone when you needed it? Explain.
- What can happen to us when we have problems but are not willing to let others help us?
- Who could you turn to right now if you needed help?

CHAIN GANG

TOPIC AREAS: Problem Solving, Working Together

CONCEPT: Dealing with problems that require concentrated effort and communicating with others is difficult. We need to learn to work with each other and to communicate in such a way that we are understood. Making wise group decisions is sometimes much harder than making individual decisions.

METHOD: Classroom activity

TIME NEEDED: 20 minutes and discussion time

MATERIALS NEEDED:
- 2-3 pair of scissors for each team of five
- 2-3 long strips (about 2 feet in length) of masking tape for each team
- 20 sheets of scrap paper for each team
- 1 blindfold for each person

ACTIVITY: Divide your group into teams of five. Have them sit down on the floor in a circle or around a table. Give each team a stack of paper, 2-3 pair of scissors and 2-3 long strips of masking tape. Use the blindfolds to tie each team's wrists together. They should now be sitting side-by-side in a circle with their wrists tied together. Tie their wrists tight enough that they have to work together to use their hands, but not so tight that the blood is cut off to the hands.

Explain that the object of this activity is to work as a team to create the longest chain using paper and masking tape. The chain is just like the ones kids make out of construction paper at Christmas time and put on their Christmas tree. Decide on a time limit. I like to use about eight to ten minutes. Every minute call out how much time they have left in the activity. At the end of the allowed time, compare chains to see which team has the longest one.

VARIATIONS: Instead of tying their hands together, make them keep one hand behind their back throughout the activity. If you choose this variation, have half of the people on each team use the hand that they don't write with. You could also blindfold some of the team members. Be sure that you don't blindfold the ones using the scissors. Another option is to make them go through this activity without talking.

DISCUSSION IDEAS:
- What problems did you encounter?
- How did you solve the problems?
- Did the activity get easier as you went along? Explain.
- What procedures did you use to work together?
- Did any of you observe other groups and make changes based on what you saw? Explain.
- Is it OK to get ideas from others when trying to solve a problem? Why or why not?
- Did your group choose a leader? How did you choose one? How did it work if you didn't choose one? Do you wish you had chosen a leader?
- What would you do differently if you were to repeat this activity?
- What effect did the calling out of how much time you had left have on your group?

- How can this activity relate to other activities in your life?
- What can you learn about working with others from this activity?

CILIA ON STRIKE

TOPIC AREA: Tobacco

CONCEPT: As a person smokes, tar is sucked into the lungs. As a matter of fact, if you were to smoke one pack of cigarettes a day for one year, you would inhale approximately one quart of tar. This tar travels down the air passage on it's way to the lungs. When the tar reaches the lungs, it is deposited in the tiny air sacks and will eventually fill them up. This will lead to diminished breathing capacity and eventually emphysema.

There are tiny hairs located in the air passage called cilia. They protect the lungs from foreign particles such as tar. To accomplish this task, the cilia wave back and forth and capture the tar on hair-like strands. When the cilia become too coated with tar to wave back and forth anymore, they can not do their job. At this point the tar proceeds directly to the lungs without any of it being intercepted by the cilia.

METHOD: Classroom activity

TIME NEEDED: 20 minutes

MATERIALS NEEDED:
- One inflatable beach ball for every 10 - 15 people

ACTIVITY: Divide your group into teams of ten to fifteen people. Give each team an inflated beach ball. Tell them that you want them to see how many times they can hit the ball in the air before it hits the ground.

Record how many times each group was able to hit the ball.

For round two, the object is the same but there is an additional rule. Before anyone may hit the ball twice, everyone must hit the ball once. Once again record how many times each group was able to hit the ball.

In round three, they are still trying to see how many times they can hit the ball. This time everyone may hit it as many times as they like, but no one may move their feet to hit the ball. Record how many times each group was able to hit the ball.

For round number four, the object is the same. However, not only may they not move their feet, they may only use one arm to hit the ball. They must decide before the round starts which arm they will use. They must place the arm they aren't going to use behind their back or in their pocket and only hit the ball with the other arm. Record how many times each group was able to hit the ball.

DISCUSSION IDEAS:
* Compare how the teams did in the various rounds.
* How did your group do in the first round?
* How did your group do when everyone had to hit the ball before someone could hit it again?
* How hard was it when you couldn't move? How did your group do when you couldn't move your feet and could only hit with one arm?
* How can we compare this activity with the slowing down of the cilia in our air passage?
* How does this activity show the effect that tar has on the cilia?

- Was it harder or easier as more restrictions were placed on the group? Explain.
- What happens to your lungs when the cilia become coated with tar?

COME ON SIX

TOPIC AREA: Stress

CONCEPT: Stress is not something that usually comes on full force all at one time. In most cases it is a gradual building kind of thing that you hardly notice. Your stress might be caused by a number of things that build up or it could be just one future event which looms larger and larger the closer it gets. We could use a test at school as an example. When it is announced that you will be having a test in a couple of weeks you may feel some stress but two weeks seems like a long way off at the time. As the date of the test grows nearer, your stress level begins to increase and you may start exhibiting both physical and emotional signs of stress. This anticipation causes anxiety and increases the closer to the event you get.

METHOD: Classroom activity

TIME NEEDED: 20 minutes and discussion time

MATERIALS NEEDED:
- 1 piece of paper per person
- 1 pencil or pen per group of five
- 1 dice per group

ACTIVITY: Divide you group into groups of five. It is best if they are sitting around a table, but the activity can be played on the floor. Each person needs to have a piece of paper and each group needs to have one pen or pencil and one dice.

The activity works likes this. Any person in the group may be the one to start by rolling the dice. The object is to roll a six. Each person gets one roll of the dice to roll a six. If the person does not roll a six, then the dice is passed to the person on their left and they have one roll to try and get a six. This pattern continues until someone rolls a six. Upon rolling a six, that person takes the pencil and starts to number on their piece of paper from 1 to 100. (You can adjust this number for groups of varying abilities.) The rules are that the numbers must be written one a time, in consecutive order and they must be legible. Have the person who is writing count out loud as they are writing each number. This tends to increase the excitement and stress of the activity. Everyone else keeps rolling the dice, skipping the person who is writing.

The person continues to write numbers until someone else in the group rolls a six. At this time, they must stop writing and give the pencil to that person who now begins to write. Remember that the dice continues around the table as the person is writing. When your turn to write is over, you once again take your turn rolling the dice.

Each time an individual rolls a six, they continue to write numbers from where they left off. For example, if you had written numbers 1 to 15 on your first turn then you would pick up with number 16 the next time you rolled a six. The round continues until someone in the group reaches 100. I would suggest that you have at least two rounds.

DISCUSSION IDEAS:
- How easy was it for you to roll a six?
- How high did you get in writing numbers?

- How easy was it to get the pencil when it was your turn to write? Did this change as the game got closer to the end? How?
- When the activity first began, what was the level of excitement in your group?
- How did the excitement level change as people got closer to 100?
- How can we compare this activity to stress in our lives?
- How anxious do we feel about something that is going to happen a year down the road?
- How does our anxiety level change the closer the event is to happening?
- Please describe a situation where you or a friend were stressed out over something that wasn't too bad when it actually happened.
- Do we sometimes cause ourselves to become stressed when we don't really need to be? Explain.
- What are some of the behaviors that we exhibit when we are under stress?
- How does our behavior affect others?
- What are some of the negative ways that we can reduce our anxiety or stress level about future events? (Tests, sporting events, an oral report, dating, getting a job, college, etc.)
- What are some of the positive ways that we can reduce our anxiety or stress level about future events? (See question above)
- How can we help others reduce their levels of stress?

CONCENTRATION

TOPIC AREA: Drugs (Marijuana)

CONCEPT: One of the effects of marijuana on the body is short term memory loss. You have a harder time remembering things that you have learned or heard recently. This is a problem when you want to study for a test, complete a complex task, participate in sports, hold down a job, play a musical instrument, etc. Marijuana can stay in the body for up to a month; therefore, a weekend smoker never really recovers from his/her drug use.

METHOD: Classroom activity

TIME NEEDED: 30 minutes and discussion time

MATERIALS NEEDED:
- An empty wall, blackboard, whiteboard or a large piece of paper that can be taped to the wall to prevent damage to the wall
- 12 pairs of playing cards
- Masking tape

ACTIVITY: You will need to use rows of playing cards to create a game board on the blackboard with the playing cards. Lightly tape the cards face down against the blackboard. Make the rows six cards horizontally and four cards vertically. (If you need the game to be easier, make your rectangle smaller by using less cards) Mix them up as you tape them to the blackboard. When finished you should have twelve pairs of cards on the blackboard. You will need to identify each row, both ver-tically and horizontally. Down the left side of the rec-tangle write the letters A, B, C and D; next to each row and across the top, write the numbers one through six. This will create the format for the game of concentra-tion.

Divide your group into two teams. No one may have paper or something to write with. One team should be facing the playing cards and the other team should turn around facing away from the playing cards so they can't see them. Each team needs a team captain. Have it be the person whose birthday is closest to yours. You will accept answers only from the team captain, but every-one on the team can help decide which cards to turn over. This position can be rotated throughout the game. The object of the game is to see which team can match the most cards. They receive one point for each pair suc-cessfully matched up. You may allow three minutes for each team to plan their strategy for remembering where the cards are located if you would like to discuss "work-ing together" after the game is over.

The game starts by having the team facing the board ask for two cards to be turned over. To indicate which cards, they must call out the row number and the alphabet letter. When the card is turned over, you will call out what card has been shown. Be sure that each team, especially the team facing backwards, hears the row number location, row letter location and the name of each playing card you turn over. They will now pick a second card. If the cards match, then they get a point and the two cards stay turned face up. I usually allow the facing away team an extra turn if they call a card which has already been matched and turned face up. If either team does get a match, then they take another turn. The game continues until all the cards have been matched up in pairs.

When the score shows that the game is halfway over, have the teams switch positions. This will give both teams the chance to experience facing away from the cards. The obvious problem is that the team which has their backs turned to the board must remember which cards have been turned over and memorize their location without the benefit of looking at the cards. The only description of the board they receive is from the teacher as the cards are turned over.

DISCUSSION IDEAS:
- How easy was the game to play?
- What problems did the facing team have?
- What problems did the facing away team have?
- How difficult was it to have the team agree on which cards to choose?
- How hard was it for the facing team to remember where the cards were?
- How hard was it for the facing away team to remember where the cards were?
- What did each team do to try and remember where the cards were?
- How well did your plan work to remember where the cards were?
- Did you change your plan during the game? Explain.
- How can the facing away team be compared to a person who is a marijuana smoker?
- In what ways could this handicap a person in their activities or school work?
- What impact would this effect have on a person who has a job?

- In what types of activities or jobs would this effect be harmful?
- How would your life be changed if you had trouble with your short term memory?

CRYSTAL BALL

TOPIC AREA: Decision Making

CONCEPT: Knowledge is power. The more you know about a subject or situation, the better decisions you can make. This is true in the area of alcohol and other drug use, teen sexuality, gang membership and many other areas of a kid's life. We need to convince our students that they need to have all of the facts before they engage in behaviors that can be harmful or self-destructive. The more facts you have, the easier it is to make decisions that will not hurt you in the short or long term.

METHOD: Classroom demonstration

TIME NEEDED: 10 minutes and discussion time

MATERIALS NEEDED:
- 5 sheets of paper with specified numbers on them

ACTIVITY: This is a great activity to show how smart the teacher is. You will need to prepare five sheets of paper in advance of this demonstration. Label the papers "A" through "E". Make the pieces of paper large enough so that everyone in the class can read the numbers on the pages from their seats. On each page write the following numbers. Put the numbers in sequential order. They may be put in vertical or horizontal lines. The purpose of putting them in sequential order and in lines is to make it easier for your students to find specific numbers when you do the demonstration.

Page "A"
1, 3, 5, 7, 9, 11, 13, 15, 17, 19, 21, 23, 25, 27, 29, 31.

Page "B"
2, 3, 6, 7, 10, 11, 14, 15, 18, 19, 22, 23, 26, 27, 30, 31.

Page "C"
4, 5, 6, 7, 12, 13, 14, 15, 20, 21, 22, 23, 28, 29, 30, 31.

Page "D"
8, 9, 10, 11, 12, 13, 14, 15, 24, 25, 26, 27, 28, 29, 30, 31

Page "E"
16, 17, 18, 19, 20, 21, 22, 23, 24, 25, 26, 27, 28, 29, 30, 31.

Start the demonstration by asking one of the students in your group to think what their birthday is. Turn around so you can't see the person and have them tell the rest of the class what their birthday is. Be sure that they do it in such a fashion that you can not hear what the date is. Now turn back around and show that person the sheet of numbers marked "A". Ask them if their birth date is shown on that sheet. If the student answers "no," then go on to the next sheet. If the student answers "yes" then remember the first number shown on that page. Continue this process through the rest of the pages marked "B" through "E". If the student answers "no" on any page, then you can just go to the next page. However, each time they answer "yes", you need to add the first number on the page to the first number on any other page that they answered "yes" to. When you have gone through all of the pages, you will have added up the first number on each of the pages that they answered "yes" to. This total will be the date of their birthday.

Let's try an example: The birth date of the person you have chosen is the 13th. They do not tell you this number, but they do tell the rest of the group. Starting with the page marked "A", you ask if their birth date is on this page. The number 13 is on the page marked "A", so they would answer "yes". You would look at the first number listed on page "A" and remember it. The first number is a "1". Now show them the page marked "B". Ask them again if their birth date is on the page. They will answer "no". Since it is not on that page you can continue. On page "C" they would answer "yes" since the number 13 is showing on that page. Since the answer was "yes", you now need to add the first number on that page to the number that you remembered from page "A", which was a 1. You now have a total of 5. When you ask about page "D" they will again answer "yes". This means that you will add the first number of page "D" to your total of 5 for a new total of 13. You will now show them page "E". They will answer that their number is not on page "E". You have now shown them all five pages. You added the first number of each page that they said "yes" their birth date was on that page. By adding these up you have found that the correct answer for their birth date is 13. You can do this with any chosen number. I find it fun to do it with their birth date.

After going through this exercise a number of times, you can stop and ask the first few questions listed below. Then have them guess at how you were able to do this. If they can not figure out the secret, eventually you should tell them and repeat the demonstration with them knowing how to do it. You can even have one of the students be the leader of the demonstration.

DISCUSSION IDEAS:

- Were you surprised that I could guess the right birth date? Why or why not?
- Have you figured out how I am able to do this?
- Do you figure that there is a trick that I am not telling you about? Why or why not?
- How important is information when you are trying to figure something out?
- How important is it to have the right information before you make a decision?
- What effect does information have on decisions that you make?
- How do you think correct information can influence decisions that you make about alcohol and other drugs? How about sexuality or violence?
- Who can you depend on to give you correct information?
- How do you know when you are getting correct information instead of just someone's opinion?
- Which is more important: someone's opinion or the facts? Why?

The idea for this activity was suggested by Bruce Bushnell and Kevin Card. Thanks Bruce and Kevin!

DEATH TRAP

TOPIC AREA: Sexuality

CONCEPT: Since we were little children we have always been encouraged to share. In today's society we have taken this well meaning cliché and in the realm of sexual activity made it not only harmful, but deadly. Adolescents who gag at the thought of using someone else's toothbrush seem quite willing to share one of life's most intimate relationships with whomever they are "in love" with this month.

Casual sexual activity is popular among America's youth and is beginning at an increasingly earlier age. The unfortunate side effect of this rise in sexual activity is the corresponding rise in sexually transmitted diseases, including AIDS. Youth need to understand that they are not only experimenting sexually with their present partner, but also all of their partner's previous partners and their previous partners.

METHOD: Classroom activity

TIME NEEDED: 15 minutes and discussion time

MATERIALS NEEDED:
- You will need to visit your local chemistry teacher to help you with this one. Ask for two chemicals. The first is Phenolphthalein. Have it put into a bottle with an eye dropper. You won't need very much of this. The second is Sodium Hydroxide. You will want about a liter of this. It will need to be diluted. The

chemistry teacher that I worked with said that I should have you ask for a "1 molar solution." The dictionary says this is "one mole of solute per liter of solution." Don't worry about what it is, let the chemistry teacher mix it up for you.

- In addition to the two chemicals, you will need one medium size (about 10 ounces) clear plastic glass for each participant.
- Masking tape and a marking pen

ACTIVITY: Before the class, prepare a plastic glass for each participant. For every ten participants, fill one glass half way with the diluted sodium hydroxide solution. For example, if you have a group of thirty people you would fill three glasses with the diluted sodium hydroxide. Fill the rest of the plastic glasses half way with plain water.

To begin the activity, give each participant one of the plastic glasses that you prepared. *Warn them not to take a drink.* Do not indicate which glasses have sodium hydroxide and which glasses have plain water. Do not even mention that there are different liquids in the glasses. Have them write their name on a piece of masking tape and then put it on their glass.

Explain that they are to exchange liquid with three to five different people. To exchange liquid, one person pours all of their liquid into another person's glass and then pours half back into their own glass. This allows for the liquids to be completely mixed. After exchanging liquid, have them walk around the room to find the next person with whom to exchange liquid. This spreads the exchanges out around the room rather than concentrating them within one small corner of the room or group.

When all of the exchanges have been made, have the glasses placed on a table in front of the room. Now take your bottle of phenolphthalein and put one or two drops in each glass. If the water has been mixed with the sodium hydroxide, the phenolphthalein will turn a reddish color. When you have finished with all of the glasses, count up the number that turned red. Explain to the class how many glasses started out just water and how many had sodium hydroxide in them.

Even though this activity takes a lot of work to set up, it is well worth the effort. It is a very dramatic demonstration on the spread of sexually transmitted diseases. Kids are still talking about this activity months after we have done it.

DECISION MAKING TWO STEP

TOPIC AREA: Decision Making

CONCEPT: With every decision comes consequences. Consequences can be either positive or negative. In most cases, the choice that you make will determine the outcome. Before a decision is made is the time to consider all the consequences, both positive and negative. It is only after these have been considered that you can make an informed decision. There are also times that even after careful consideration, unplanned or unforeseen events can impact a decision that has been made with either positive or negative consequences that have not been anticipated. Our youth need to know that it is only by using the decision making process that they can live their lives through choice rather than by chance.

METHOD: Classroom activity

TIME NEEDED: 15 minutes and discussion time

MATERIALS NEEDED:
- Masking tape
- A penny, button, paper clip or some other small object for every two people
- Whistle
- A coin

ACTIVITY: Use masking tape to create a starting and a finishing line about 25-30 feet apart. Have everyone get a partner. Give each pair one penny or some other small object. Designate one person partner "A" and one person partner "B" in each pair. You can use height, shoe size, birth date closest to January 1st or any other method to do this.

Have all of the partner "A's" line up at the starting line. Have partner "B's" stand either behind or next to their partner. Explain that partner "B" will put their hands behind their back and place the small object in either their left or right hand. They will bring both hands out in front of them and partner "A" will try to choose which hand has the object in it.

If partner "A" guesses correctly, then he/she will take two heel-to-toe steps towards the finish line. If they guess incorrectly, then he/she must take one heel-to-toe step backwards. A heel-to-toe step is the type that is used when a police office has a DUI (Driving Under the Influence) suspect walk a line. The heel of one foot must touch the toe of the other foot as they walk. By using this method in the activity, you will guarantee that the steps they use are small ones. This guess/walk routine is repeated over and over again until partner "A" reaches the finish line.

The object is for each person to reach the finish line in the fewest rounds. A round is counted each time partner "A" makes a choice as to which hand has the object. Be sure that partner "B" keeps track of how many rounds have been played. Wait until all of the partner "A's" have finished and then check to see how many rounds were used by each partner "A". Now take them back to the starting line and have them switch roles and repeat the activity with partner "B" doing the guessing.

For added interest and discussion options, repeat

the activity and explain that this time whenever you blow the whistle everyone is to complete the round that they are on and then the next round is an "opportunity round." There are outside circumstances that they have no control over which will increase the consequences. You will then flip a coin. If it comes up heads then the next round will have double the consequences and if it comes up tails the next round will have triple the consequences. They will take four or six steps forward or two or three steps backwards depending on the result of their decision.

DISCUSSION IDEAS:
- How well did you do choosing the correct hand?
- What criteria did you use to make your decision?
- How many of you had a lot of right choices?
- How many of you had a lot of wrong choices?
- How many of you went backwards behind the starting line?
- How did the "opportunity round" impact your progress?
- How can we compare this activity to decisions you make?
- How difficult is it to make a decision? Explain.
- What are some of the decisions you make?
- What are the positive and negative consequences that could result from some of the decisions you make?
- Do some decisions have both negative and positive consequences? If so, how do you make your decision?
- What kinds of beyond-your-control events can effect the consequences?
- Can these events be either positive or negative? Explain.

- How do you know when you have enough information to make an informed decision?
- Where can you go to get additional information to help you make a decision?
- What kinds of people would be helpful to get information from?
- What kinds of people would not be helpful to get information from?

EARTHQUAKE

TOPIC AREAS: Problem Solving, Working Together

CONCEPT: Making decisions based on facts that are presented to you is an every day occurrence. Sometimes you have an over abundance of information and other times you have very little on which to base your decision. Decisions made with a group are even harder to make due to the vested interest of those in the group. However, these situations give you a good opportunity to express your opinion and present whatever reasoning you have used to reach your conclusions. This activity will help to foster those skills.

I like this activity because it goes beyond other such activities that have only the decision making component. You will see that individuals are assigned roles to play. This helps to make the simulation even more realistic, since now you have to also deal with body size and a person representing each role. It adds another component that simulations such as "Life Raft" or "Airplane" do not have. There is a physical activity involved. Instead of just eliminating people, the group can work to "save" everyone.

METHOD: Classroom activity

TIME NEEDED: 25 minutes and discussion

MATERIALS NEEDED:
- 1 copy of the story for each person

- 1 role description for each person
- 1 piece of paper or cardboard for each team of seven. The paper should be small enough that the activity is a challenge for them. I use a regular sheet of notebook paper for my groups. You can increase or decrease the size depending upon the ability level of your kids. Don't make the paper too large, you want them to have to decide who to leave out
- A watch with a second hand

ACTIVITY: Divide your group into teams of seven. Hand out one copy of the story to each person. If a group has less than seven people, you may eliminate a role. Read the story and have them follow along as you read. When you finish the story, give each group seven strips of paper. On each strip of paper have one role described. Whichever role a person chooses, that is the role they will assume in the activity. Give each group one piece of paper that represents the light fixture cover. Remind them that for a group member to not be effected by the chemical, they must not be touching the floor. The entire group must be off the floor for the same thirty seconds. Each group may ask you to time them when they are ready. They must complete the activity within the fifteen minute time limit.

GROUP ROLES:
Tour Guide - 23 years old with three young children. Your spouse has died and you are the sole financial and emotional support for the children. You hope to save enough money to go to college and become a lawyer.

Doctor - 50 years old. You have been doing research for the past ten years on a cure for AIDS. You feel that an answer is only a few months away. You have been working on the project without any other research assistant. High School Math Teacher - 32 years old. You have developed a new system of teaching that makes learning fun and interesting. You have just started to put together a training program that can be used by school districts everywhere. The system has shown great advances in student achievement levels.

Corporate Executive - 35 years old. The company employs 10,000 people. You were the key person in starting the company. The company is faced with massive layoffs unless a new product can be found. You believe such a product has been found, but the details have not been worked out yet.

Scientist - 65 years old. You have been working on the space program for 30 years. You are the key individual for the space station project. You have been working on the air recycling system for the space station. Just before leaving for a conference you told the other staff members that an answer had been found. You would tell them your findings right after the United Nations conference.

Counselor - 25 years old. You have been working with abused children. This is a group of about fifteen severely emotionally disturbed kids. You have made tremendous progress with them. Without your support, the children will probably regress and never make it outside the hospital.

General - 60 years old. You are the head of the United States Armed Forces Central Command. You know all of the national defense plans in case of a war or emergency. You are the only one that the President of the

United States has trusted to work out a military compromise with North Korea that so far has averted a war.
You are the only person that North Korea will deal with.

TRAPPED

You are part of a group from the United States that is
attending a United Nations conference on world problems. The group is touring a biological research facility.
While the group is waiting in a completely bare room for
some equipment to be brought to them, the building
begins to shake and an alarm sounds. The doors to the
room shut and lock automatically and your group is
trapped. The earthquake causes a storage container in
the next room to begin leaking. The storage container
holds a liquid biological weapon that was left over from
previous military research. When it comes in contact
with human skin it causes permanent blindness, a one
year loss of speech and a three year paralysis from the
neck down. The chemical easily passes through clothing, including shoes.

There is enough liquid in the storage container to
seep under the door and completely cover the floor of the
room that you are in with a thin film of chemical. It will
take about fifteen minutes for the entire floor to be covered. As the liquid begins to spread, the tour guide takes
out a pocket knife and pries off the cover of the light fixture. The cover is made of a material that can't be bent
or cut but can withstand the effects of the chemical. The
only problem is that the light cover is very small. Your
group must figure out how many people you can protect
by having them stand on the light cover. The chemical
is dangerous for only a short period of time. If you can
keep the people in your group from touching the floor
for a period of thirty seconds, they will be safe. Anyone

who touches the floor after the liquid has reached them, will become blind, mute and paralyzed. How many of your group can you protect? If not everyone, then which ones will you protect? What strategy will you use to get people on the light cover? Hurry, there are only fifteen minutes left for your group to make and carry out your plans!

DISCUSSION IDEAS:
- How did your team decide which people would definitely be saved?
- How did you feel about the person whose role you played?
- Which people did you make your top priority people?
- Which people did you make as lower priority people?
- How many were you able to save?
- What were your thoughts when you first saw the size of the piece of paper?
- What techniques did you use to keep people from touching the floor?
- How many different techniques did you try before you settled on one?
- Was there a leader chosen in your group? How were they chosen?
- Did everyone have input into the decisions? Explain.
- If we were to repeat this activity is there anything you would do differently?
- How can we compare this activity to decisions you make with groups you hang around with?
- Are group decisions harder to make than individual decisions? Why or why not?

EXPLODING ANSWERS

TOPIC AREA: Review Method

CONCEPT: When you are finished with a body of information, you want to have the kids review. This time of reviewing can become boring and tedious. Kids stop listening and therefore miss the benefits associated with the review time. Use this game to make the review time fun yet educational. I have used this with alcohol and other drug facts, but it can be used with any number of topics.

METHOD: Classroom activity

TIME NEEDED: Depends on the number of questions you want to ask.

MATERIALS NEEDED:
- One chair for each participant
- Four extra chairs
- Two small balloons for each question you ask plus a few extras.

ACTIVITY: Divide your group into two equal teams. If you have an extra person, assign them to be a judge. Set the activity up with two rows of chairs facing each other with the two rows about eight feet apart. If finding chairs is a problem, have the teams stand in two rows facing each other or sit on the floor. At both ends of the rows, place two chairs side-by-side. These chairs will be facing the rows and about three feet from the end of the rows. You have now formed a loose rectangle.

Have each person take a seat in one of the chairs that form the long rows. If they are standing or sitting on the floor, they should still be directly across from another person. Have both teams count off so that the people across from each other have the same number. Now place a blown up balloon on each of the two empty chairs at each end of the rows. Designate one set of two chairs as "FALSE" and the other set of two chairs as "TRUE". If you would like to label the chairs you may, although this makes the game easier.

Now you are ready to play. You will read a "TRUE/FALSE" statement to the group. Then you will call a number. The two people with that number will walk quickly to the designated TRUE/FALSE chair and pop the balloon by sitting on it. Running calls for the person to be disqualified. This will ensure some degree of safety. The popped balloon will indicate their answer. If they pop the "false" balloon then of course they have answered "false". The first person to pop the balloon, must repeat the statement if it was a true statement and they must say the statement correctly if it was a false statement. They do not have to repeat it word-for-word, but they must give you the proper concept. This makes sure they are listening and reinforces the information.

If they are wrong by having popped the wrong balloon or they can't repeat the statement, then the other person may try. If they get it right on the first try, then their team is awarded two points. If the second person answers the question or repeats the statement correctly, they receive one point for their team. If neither one of them gets it right, send them back to their seats, put out new balloons and call another number. Yes, you are right, they will know which end to go to , but they will still have to repeat the correct answer. Do not read the question again. This keeps everyone on the team awake.

Once the question is correctly answered, put new balloons on the chairs and go to the next question. Keep track of the numbers that you call so you can try to include as many people as possible. Warn everyone to keep their feet out of the walking area so no one trips. If this is a problem, either stop the game or remove those who are the offenders.

DISCUSSION IDEAS:
* This activity does not have discussion questions since it is a review technique.

EYES ON THE BALL

TOPIC AREA: Goal Setting

CONCEPT: Setting a goal is a very personal thing. If we are trying to accomplish a goal that someone else has set for us, our motivation is not as great as it would be if we set it ourselves. We also need to have our goals prioritized. All of us have more than one goal in life. We have daily goals, short term goals and long term goals. When one of these goals conflicts with another one, we need to know which one is the more important. Prioritizing will help us to make decisions that are consistent with our future success.

METHOD: Classroom activity

TIME NEEDED: 15 minutes and discussion time

MATERIALS NEEDED:
• 1 tennis ball per person

ACTIVITY: Give each person in your group a tennis ball. On the count of three have them all throw their ball into the air. The ball must go at least ten feet over their heads, but not more than fifteen feet. Have each person catch the ball that they threw. Count the number of balls that hit the ground. Try this about three times to see how they do.

For the next part of the activity explain that each person is to catch a ball that they did not throw. Once again when all the balls have come down, count the number of them that are on the ground. The object is to catch as many of the thrown balls as possible. Repeat this activity three or four times and see if the group improves.

If at this point the group has not stopped and made suggestions on how this can be accomplished, you should stop the group and ask them if they can think of ways to improve the number of thrown balls caught. Do not lead this problem solving, let the kids work it out for themselves. Let them have a couple of more tries to improve their success rate.

DISCUSSION IDEAS:
- How hard was it to catch a ball you threw yourself?
- How did the group do when catching the balls thrown by themselves?
- How hard was it to catch a ball thrown by someone else?
- How did the group do when catching a ball thrown by someone else?
- Did the group make any changes that made catching the balls easier?
- If you were to repeat this activity what changes would you make to make the number of balls caught higher?
- How can we relate this activity to goal setting?
- How easy is it to accomplish a goal that someone else sets for you?
- How easy is it to accomplish a goal that you set for yourself?
- How hard is it to have a large number of goals at one time?
- If you zero in on just one goal, is it easier or harder to accomplish that goal? Explain.

- Should goals be really easy to accomplish or really hard? Explain.
- Should goals be something you can accomplish in a short period of time?

FAIR WEATHER FRIENDS

TOPIC AREAS: Cliques, Relationships

CONCEPT: The basis of who our friends are, who we hang around with and who is part of our group is too many times decided by how we look rather than who we are. People are sought after and accepted into a group or as friends by how popular they are without any real consideration of what is on the inside.

METHOD: Classroom demonstration

TIME NEEDED: 5 minutes and discussion time

MATERIALS NEEDED:
* Book: Charlie the Caterpillar by Dom Deluise. Published by Simon & Schuster The ISBN reference number that can be used at the bookstore is 0-671-79607-0. It is available in paperback.

ACTIVITY: Read the story to your group. Be sure and show them the pictures. Don't be afraid to use this activity with older youth or hard core kids. I have found them to be very receptive to stories.

DISCUSSION IDEAS:
* How was Charlie treated when he was a caterpillar?
* How did this make Charlie feel?
* What was the reason given that the other animals didn't want to play with Charlie?
* Did Charlie have any control over how he looked?

- What happened when he became a beautiful butter-fly?
- How did this make Charlie feel?
- Why did the other animals want to be his friend now?
- Why did Charlie become Katie's friend?
- How was that friendship different than what the other animals wanted?
- How can this story relate to groups that you know?
- Have you ever known anyone like Charlie?
- How do you think they felt?
- What are the characteristics of a real friend?
- What should we look for when we are choosing groups to hang out with?
- How can we help others who are not popular?

FINGERPRINTS

TOPIC AREAS: Diversity, Self-Esteem

CONCEPT: We are all unique and have different qualities that make us special. It is this being different that allows our society to function as well as it does. Without differences, we would not have the combination of abilities and varying insights to invent and create the things that we need. We need to celebrate these differences and unique characteristics.

METHOD: Classroom activity

TIME NEEDED: 10 minutes and discussion time

MATERIALS NEEDED:
- #2 (or softer) pencil for each person
- 3 inches of clear tape for each person
- 2 pieces of blank white paper about 3 inches by 3 inches for each person

ACTIVITY: Begin by having each person use a pencil and color a space a little larger than their thumb print on a white piece of paper. They should use a lot of lead when coloring. Be sure to use a soft leaded pencil. Have them turn the pencil so the side of the lead can also be used. Be sure that the area is heavily coated with lead. Now have them take their thumb and press it down firmly on the lead covered area. They should roll the thumb firmly so that the entire area where the fingerprint is located is thoroughly covered with lead.

Now have each student take a piece of clear tape and put it on the thumb over the fingerprint area. Be sure that the tape is put on smoothly for best results. Once the tape has been placed on the thumb, take it off the thumb and put it on a clean white sheet of paper. On the paper you will be able to see the fingerprint of the thumb through the tape. Anywhere the tape was not smooth on the thumb, a clear area will be left.

Have people go around the room and compare their fingerprints with those of others. You may repeat this activity using other fingers in addition to the thumb.

DISCUSSION IDEAS:
- What do you notice about your fingerprint?
- Do you notice anything that stands out and is easily recognizable on your fingerprint? Explain.
- How does your fingerprint compare with those of others?
- How can we compare fingerprints to the characteristics of people?
- Is everyone unique? Explain.
- Fingerprints are hard to see. What are some characteristics that are easy to see?
- How do these characteristics help to make everyone different?
- Why would it be important to have different types of people in the world?
- Why is it important to have different types of people in your town or city?
- Why is it important to have different types of people in your school?
- Why is it important to have different types of people as your friends?

- What are certain characteristics that make people special?
- If we were all the same, what kind of a world would we have? Explain.
- What does being different add to the world around you?
- How does being unique make you special?
- Do people always recognize how special each of us are? Explain.
- How does being different help us sometimes and hurt us sometimes?

The idea for this activity was suggested by Jon Wingate. Thanks, Jon!

FRUIT SALAD

TOPIC AREA: Stress

CONCEPT: Kids have a lot of stress in their lives today. Some of it is just the ordinary, everyday kinds of things that we have to deal with on a regular basis. Other times the stressors that they face are of a more difficult nature. On occasion they may face a situation that is overwhelming such as a death or divorce in the family, moving schools or communities, a relationship change or other major event. Each of these levels of stress needs to be dealt with in a different manner. The same techniques that are used to handle daily stress will not satisfactorily handle other kinds of stress. Stress management techniques must be explored to cover all types of situations.

METHOD: Classroom activity

TIME NEEDED: 20 minutes and discussion time

MATERIALS NEEDED:
- 2 spoons for each team of five
- A variety of fruits and vegetables. Enough for each participant to have two. They should be of a variety of sizes and shapes.
- A table (optional)
- Masking tape

ACTIVITY: Divide your group into teams of five. The activity is set up as a relay race. Indicate a starting line with the masking tape. The distance from the starting line to the table area should be about fifteen to twenty feet. Give each team 2 spoons and have them line up single file behind the starting line. At the other end of the room, put ten fruits and vegetables on a table or on the floor in front of each team. Each team gets their own set of ten fruits or vegetables. The fruits and vegetables should be of various sizes and shapes. Teams should not have any duplicate items in front of them. Some suggestions for items are apples, oranges, bananas, carrots, grapes, onions, cucumbers, melons, fresh string beans, or any other item that has an unusual shape or size.

The activity begins with the first person on each team having a spoon. They walk up to the pile of fruits and vegetables and pick one of them up and place it on the spoon. They may pick any item. Subsequent team members may also pick any item that has not been carried by their team. Do not set the order for them to pick, let that be part of their decision. Once the item is on the spoon, they may not touch it with their hands. They must walk back to their team and transfer the item to the spoon of the next person in line. The items must be transferred without the use of their hands. If the item is dropped they may pick it up with their hands and put it back on the original spoon to try again. They will then walk it back up to the table and place it in a new pile. They must keep the piles separate so they know which ones they have carried already. If it falls off while walking, they must pick it up with their hand and return to whichever end they just left, place it on the spoon and begin again. Each team member must go to the back of the line and take a second turn. This will allow each team member to experience two different sizes and shapes during the relay. They will also have a harder object the second time around since the easy shapes and sizes will go during the first round.

I would suggest that you repeat the activity twice. On the second time through, if you don't have identical piles, have them switch to a new pile of fruits and vegetables. This will give them a slightly different experience.

VARIATION: If you don't want to use fruits and vegetables, this activity can be done with various items that you find around the house or your classroom. Just be sure they are of different sizes, shapes, and weights.

DISCUSSION IDEAS:
* How hard was the activity for you?
* How did you choose which item you were going to carry?
* How difficult was it to keep the items on the spoon?
* Which items were easy to carry?
* Which items were hard to carry?
* If you were to repeat this activity, what would you do differently?
* How could this activity be compared to different stressors in your life?
* What are some of the things that cause stress in your life?
* Is stress always bad? Explain.
* Do all things that happen to you cause you the same level of stress? Why or why not?
* What are some of the techniques that you can use to take care of the small daily stressors?
* What are some of the techniques you could use to take care of major stressors?
* Are there ever stressors that need another person to help you? Describe them.
* What type of a person would you go to ask for help with a major stressor?

FUMBLE FINGERS

TOPIC AREAS: Alcohol, Drugs

CONCEPT: When a person uses any kind of a drug, it has an effect on the body. When alcohol or another depressant-type drug is used, the body will react by slowing down its functions. When these functions are impaired in such a manner, it becomes more difficult for a person to complete certain tasks. This is especially true for tasks which require manual dexterity.

METHOD: Classroom activity

TIME NEEDED: 15 minutes and discussion time

MATERIALS NEEDED:
- 1 pair of gloves for each team of five
- 2 chocolate Hershey Kisses for each person plus a few extras
- A watch with a second hand

ACTIVITY: Divide your group into teams of five. This will be a relay race, so if your group doesn't have equal teams, have one person on each team without five members go twice. Line the teams up behind a starting line. Place five Hershey Kisses on a chair, a table or the floor, fifteen feet or so in front of the starting line. All the teams will start at the same time. The object is for each person to walk up to the kisses, unwrap one of them and eat it. They do not have to eat the candy before they leave the chair or table. They may put the candy in their mouth and eat it as they walk back to the line. However, it must be completely unwrapped before they leave the chair or table. If for some reason the individual does not like Hershey Kisses or just does not care to eat it, they may leave the unwrapped candy on the chair or table and return to their team. When they return, the next person leaves the starting line. You will need to time each team. Record how much time it takes each team to accomplish this task.

Now for the second round, repeat the same activity except for the fact that each person must wear a pair of gloves when they are unwrapping the Hershey Kiss. Have the last person in line come up to the front of the line and turn to face the first person. The person who was last in line is given the pair of gloves. When you say "Go" they will put the pair of gloves on the first person in line and then return to the end of the line. The first person, which now has a pair of gloves on, goes up and unwraps the candy. When they return, they put the gloves on the next person in line. This process continues throughout the round so that no one puts the gloves on themselves. Once again record the amount of time it takes for each team to accomplish this task. Record the scores and compare how quickly each team accomplished the task in the second round as opposed to how quickly they finished it in the first round.

DISCUSSION IDEAS:
- How difficult was it to unwrap the kiss without the gloves on?
- How difficult was it to unwrap the kiss with the gloves on?
- In what way did the gloves make the task harder?
- Did some people find it harder than others to unwrap the candy kiss?

- How can this activity be compared to the use of alcohol and other drugs?
- What activities would be harder for you to accomplish in your daily life if you were impaired?
- What problems would you have if you were impaired on the job?
- Are some people affected by drugs to a greater degree than others? Why or why not?
- Even if you don't use drugs, how can their use by others affect your life?
- How do impaired people effect others around them?
- How easy is it for you to get your work done if you have to help an impaired person complete their work and still do yours?
- What kind of help from other people does someone who is impaired need?
- If you noticed someone at your school impaired by drugs, what would you do? What would be the results of your actions?

FUNNY BONE

TOPIC AREA: Diversity

CONCEPT: We all like different things. That does not make some of us right and others of us wrong. Liking different things allows us to have dozens and dozens of cereals lining the shelves of the supermarket. It is what drives the advertising and clothing industry. No one would argue that we should all be clones of each other, that is until we start talking about culture, ethnicity, appearance, etc. Then we begin to stereotype those who are different than ourselves. We also become very judgmental of anything that smacks of difference. Our kids needs to understand that differences are OK and that just because someone likes to dress or look a certain way, it does not make that person inherently bad or worth less to society.

METHOD: Classroom activity

TIME NEEDED: 20 minutes and discussion time

MATERIALS NEEDED:
- 1 newspaper page of comics for each participant, plus a few extras. The pages must be from different days.
- Scissors (1 pair for every 5-6 people)
- Masking tape
- A pencil and paper for each participant

ACTIVITY: You will need to bring in a page of comics from the newspaper for each participant. You will need to collect these over a number of days since each participant needs a completely different set of comics. Pass out the pages. Explain that you want each person to determine which comic on their page is the funniest one for that day. If a person just can't find any one on the page that is funny, have a few extra pages for them to look over. After they have found the one that is funny to them, have them post it on the wall with masking tape. On the masking tape write a number or letter so people can designate one from another. Once everyone has posted the comic strip that they think is funny, have each person make a list from one to however many you have and rank the comics from the funniest to the least funny. Compare results.

DISCUSSION IDEAS:

- How difficult was it to select a funny comic strip to place on the wall?
- How hard was it to rank the comics from really funny to not so funny?
- How did your choices compare to the class choices?
- Should everyone agree on the same comic? Why or why not?
- Does it make any difference what anyone else thinks if you don't agree?
- How do many different opinions on the same topic help make our society a better place to live?
- What would happen if we all agreed on everything?
- If someone disagrees with you, are they a bad person?
- How does our background help shape how we think?
- Should we ignore our background when we are looking at various issues? Explain.
- Should we judge others as less than ourselves just because of the way they think or act? Explain.

GLACIERS

TOPIC AREA: Addiction

CONCEPT: Alcohol and other drug use have long term effects. Things happen to your body over a period of time. Certain factors, such as increased use or use at a young age can speed up the occurrence of these effects. Even if we can't see the effects taking place, they are still happening within our body, no matter how slowly. Over time the results of this damage will begin to show. Circumstances such as being genetically predisposed to addiction or using drugs that have certain characteristics can also speed up addiction or bodily effects.

METHOD: Classroom activity

TIME NEEDED: 10 minutes and discussion time

MATERIALS NEEDED:
- 1 ice cube per team of three
- 1 roll of paper towels
- 1 watch with a second-hand

ACTIVITY: Divide your group into teams of three. Give each team an ice cube. Explain that the activity consists of seeing how long it takes each team to completely melt their ice cube. They may only use their hands and breath to melt the ice cube. They may not rub it on the floor or on their clothes. As each team finishes, have them raise their hands and you call out their finishing time.

DISCUSSION IDEAS:

*   What did you find to be the best method for melting the ice cube?
*   What problems did your team have?
*   How cold was the ice cube when you first started? After you got going did it stop feeling as cold? Explain. (Once your skin becomes numb you don't feel the effects as much)
*   Why didn't all the teams finish melting their ice cubes at the same time?
*   How could this activity apply to addiction?
*   How could this activity apply to long term effects of alcohol and other drugs?
*   List some circumstances or behaviors that increase the speed at which alcohol and other drugs can harm us.
*   Can you always tell what effect a drug is having on your body? Explain.

GRAB IT!

TOPIC AREA: Alcohol

CONCEPT: When alcohol is in your system, you can not react as quickly to events around you or perform as well. Judgment, thinking speed and reaction time are just some of the areas that are affected. This slowing down of the brain can cause automobile accidents, poor decisions, and poor school or job performance.

METHOD: Classroom activity

TIME NEEDED: 20 minutes and discussion time

MATERIALS NEEDED:
- You will need something that comes in three different colors. I have used poker chips since they come in red, blue and white. I have also used different colored construction paper, marbles, spray painted rocks, etc. You will need about thirty items for each group of eight. Have different amounts of each color. Maybe 5 red poker chips, 10 blue chips and 15 white chips.
- 1 pair of dice for each group.
- Masking tape

ACTIVITY: Divide into groups of eight. Use the masking tape to make a three foot square on the floor. Have the group of eight divide into two teams of four. Place one player from each team on each side of the square. Spread out your thirty items at random in the square. Choose one player to begin the game. Give him/her the pair of dice. They are to roll the dice in the square. If the dice add up to an even number, then everyone reaches in and tries to grab as many items as they can. If the dice add up to an odd number, then no action is taken and the player rolls again. The first round continues until each player has had a chance to roll the dice.

Scoring is as follows: Designate each color to be worth a certain number of points. The most numerous color will be worth one point. The middle item is worth five points and the least number of items is worth ten points. This means that the players are trying to grab the colors that are worth the most points. Add up each team's score after each roll of the dice. If a player grabs, or even touches, any items when the dice show an odd number, then those points are deducted from the team's total score.

For round two, the rules change slightly. Everything is the same except that each person on the team which is not rolling the dice must say the phrase "Alcohol slows you down", after the dice has stopped rolling, before they may reach for any of the items. If they reach before they finish saying "Alcohol slows you down", then the points they get are subtracted from the team's total. They do not say the phrase one at a time, they all say it at the same time.

DISCUSSION IDEAS:
- How well did you do seeing if the dice added up to odd or even?
- Did it make any difference if you were the one rolling the dice? Why or why not?
- What strategy did you use to get the most points?

- How well did you do going after the high point colors?
- Did you and one of your teammates ever go after the same item?
- What difference did the new rule make about saying the phrase first?
- After saying the phrase were there many high point colors left to get?
- How can saying the phrase compare to being under the influence of alcohol?
- What are some things that you do everyday that would not be done as well if you were using alcohol?
- If your thinking process was slowed down, how would this affect your daily life?
- What impact would drinking have on your future goals? Explain.

GRASS IS GREENER

TOPIC AREA: Cliques

CONCEPT: No matter what we have, what others have sometimes looks better. This manifests itself in the desire to be a part of the "in crowd." We want to do what they do and have what they have. The result of this type of thinking has people believing that certain groups or individuals are better than others. This can affect a person's self-esteem and have an impact on behavior.

METHOD: Classroom demonstration

TIME NEEDED: 10 minutes and discussion time

MATERIALS NEEDED:
- Book: The Sneetches and Other Stories by Dr. Seuss, published by Random House

ACTIVITY: Read the story "Sneetches" to your group. Be sure to show the pictures to the kids as you read. I am always amazed at how well kids respond to stories, no matter what their age. This story is no exception.

DISCUSSION IDEAS:
- Which group thought they were the best? Why?
- Which group thought they were less important? Why?
- How did the Star-belly group treat the Plain-belly group? Describe some specific examples.
- What did Sylvester McMonkey McBean promise the Plain-bellies?

- How did his plan accomplish what the Plain-bellies wanted?
- How did the Star-bellies react to the plan?
- After McBean left, what lessons do you think the Sneetches had learned?
- Do we have any groups in our area that think they are better than other groups? Why would they think that?
- When is it good to think your group is the best?
- When is it bad to think your group is the best?
- What role does advertising or other media play in making things "in" or "out"?
- What happens to society when groups think they are better than others?
- How do people feel when they are labeled as part of the "out" group?
- How do people feel when they are labeled as part of the "in" group?
- Have you ever known someone who was part of the "in" group? Please describe. (No names)
- What effect did this have on them?
- Have you ever known someone who was part of the "out" group? Please describe. (No names)
- What effect did this have on them?

HEROES

TOPIC AREA: Role Models

CONCEPT: Everyone needs some one to look up to, to admire, to have respect for. The problem today is that many of our heroes are not always the best role models. We need to broaden the definition of hero to someone that our kids can relate to and therefore aspire to be like. They need to look around their own neighborhood and find people that have traits and lives that they admire.

METHOD: Classroom activity

TIME NEEDED: 15 minutes in class and then an over night assignment. 30 minutes more the next day and discussion time.

MATERIALS NEEDED:
• A list of questions for each participant

ACTIVITY: Break up into groups of three. Have each group brainstorm a list of at least five characteristics they would use to define a positive hero. Explain that the word "hero" does not mean someone who fought in a war or saved someone from physical harm, but rather someone who they could look up to as a role model with respect and admiration. The characteristics should be things that they can find in people they know. These are not to be physical characteristics but rather behaviors, attitudes, life-styles and personality traits that are noteworthy. Give the groups about five minutes to develop their list. Have each group read their list to the entire group. Make note of items that appear on more than one list.

Give each person a list of questions. First have them write down the person's name that they are going to interview and then write why they chose that particular person. The following questions should be included:

1. How long have you lived in this area?

2. What was your family like when you were growing up?

3. Name one person who made a big difference in your life. Why?

4. Describe an event in your life that made a big difference in how you thought or acted.

5. Describe an event in your life that gave you a great deal of satisfaction.

6. Name some people that you admire and tell me why.

7. What are some things that you would like to accomplish in the next few years?

8. What one sentence of advice would you give to someone my age?

Of course you can add more questions or delete some to meet the needs of your group. Have the students use this list to interview someone that meets the list of characteristics which the groups brainstormed. They don't have to meet all of the characteristics, but at least some of them.

The next day have them break up into groups of three and share the answers with each other that they received. When they have finished, have each person read why they chose to interview the person that they did and the one sentence of advice they were given. If the advice is antisocial, ask the class if this is positive advice or advice from someone who hasn't completely thought through what they said. Ask how the statement could be changed to make it a pro-social statement. Have the individual rephrase the statement in a pro-social format.

VARIATION: Instead of going around the room to share the one sentence of advice, have them draw a picture of the person they interviewed and write the advice at the bottom of the picture. Have them read the advice and then post the pictures around the room. If you think drawing a face is too much, then have them make a poster out of the saying and put that on the wall. This is a great visual reinforcer of the advice that they were given.

DISCUSSION IDEAS:
- How hard was it to list characteristics of a positive hero?
- Would you add or subtract any characteristics now that you have completed this activity?
- What is the difference between a positive and a negative hero?
- How hard was it for you to decide who you would interview? Why?
- How did the interview go?

- Was it easy for the person to answer your questions? Explain.
- Did you hear any answers that you didn't expect to hear? What were they?
- Which statements of advice did you think were really good? Why?
- Should all famous people be looked up to? Why or why not?
- What impact can role models have on our lives?
- How should we choose our role models?
- How would you be able to answer these same questions if they were asked of you today?
- In five years? In ten years?
- Could you be someone's hero? Why or why not?

HIGH WIRE ACT

TOPIC AREA: Alcohol

CONCEPT: The effects of alcohol on the body are many. One of the areas that is affected is depth perception. This ability to judge the distance of objects is crucial in many of our day-to-day tasks. This is especially true when it comes to driving. The ability to properly judge distances is crucial when driving a vehicle. This ability is also important when performing many of the duties in the workplace.

METHOD: Classroom activity or demonstration

TIME NEEDED: 20 minutes and discussion time

MATERIALS NEEDED;
- One pair of binoculars for each team of 5 people (The ones marked "wide angle" work the best)
- Masking tape

ACTIVITY: Divide your group into teams of five. They should line up single file with a twelve foot length of masking tape going away from them on the floor in front of each team. Begin the activity by having them walk the line using a heel-to-toe walking method. This method requires the heel of one foot to touch the toe of the other foot as the person walks the line. This is a duplication of the drunk driver's sobriety test that is given on the side of the road. Make it a relay race with one person at a time walking the line. Be sure that they use the heel-to-toe method. If they fall off the line they must come back and start again. Have the person walk up and back on the tape then have the next person take their turn. Continue until each person on the team has had a turn.

Now give each team a pair of binoculars. Have them repeat the process of walking heel- to-toe, but this time they must use one eye to look through the wrong end of the binoculars with the eye that is not looking through the lens kept closed. If they fall off the line, they must come back and start again. After they have completed walking the tape in one direction, they turn and go back to the starting line. On the return trip they are still walking heel-to-toe, but not looking through the binoculars. When they return to the starting line they give the binoculars to the next person. Continue until each person on the team has had a turn.

VARIATION: Demonstration - Use masking tape to make a line on the floor about twelve feet long. Bring a student to the front of the room and have him/her walk the line using the heel-to-toe method. After they have completed the walk, bring them back to the start of the line and give them a pair of binoculars. While looking through the binoculars with one eye open and one eye closed, have them walk the line using the same heel-to-toe method that they used before.

DISCUSSION IDEAS:
- How did you do when you walked the line without the binoculars?
- How did you do when you walked the line with the binoculars?
- What effect did the binoculars have on your ability to walk?

- What effect did the binoculars have on your ability to see?
- If you were driving, what problems would this effect have on your driving ability?
- What other activities would be hard to accomplish if your vision were distorted like this?
- What jobs in the workplace would be dangerous if your vision were distorted like this?
- Would you want to be a passenger in a car if the driver's vision were distorted like this?
- Explain.

The idea for this activity was suggested by Julie Brush. Thanks, Julie!

HOW FAR IS IT?

TOPIC AREAS: Alcohol, Drugs

CONCEPT: People have a hard time judging such things as the passage of time or how far away something is. Our perceptions of time and distance are usually incorrect and distorted. When we are impaired by alcohol or other drugs, then this problem with perception is increased. Of course the ability to accurately determine distances is crucial when you are driving a car or doing something else that requires travel. As our ability to properly measure time and distance diminishes, then our ability to operate motor vehicles, boats, bicycles and other forms of transportation is also diminished.

METHOD: Classroom activity

TIME NEEDED: 20 minutes and discussion time

MATERIALS NEEDED:
- 1 pencil or pen per person
- 1 piece of paper per person
- A watch with a second hand

ACTIVITY: Before the activity starts, go outside and measure the distance from one or more spots to five other spots. Do it in this fashion: Stand in one place and look around for a prominent object, such as a tree or the corner of a building. Now pace off the distance from where you are standing, to the object. Make the distance relatively far away, such as 100 to 300 feet. Record the distance for each object that you measured.

Rather than taking the time to measure the distance with a tape measure, just walk off the distance and count your strides. Measure one of your strides and multiply this measurement by the number of strides that you took. The measurements don't have to be exact. Measure to about five different objects. You may start from the same spot for each measurement or you may move around and use completely different areas to measure each time. If you move each time, then the activity will take longer to complete. These measurements will be used in the second half of the activity. The first half of the activity involves time.

To start the activity, be sure that each person has a pen or pencil and a piece of paper. Explain that you are going to check your watch and allow a certain amount of time to pass. You will indicate when you are starting and when you are stopping. Ask them not to count "One thousand one, one thousand two" or any other form of keeping track. What you want them to do is to write down how long they thought elapsed from the time you said start to the time you said stop. Record the amount of time you gave them.

Repeat this part of the activity with varying lengths of time about four times. When you have completed as many times as you are going to do, then go back to the first time and find out what the guesses were from your group. An easy way to do this is for you to call out a certain time and have them raise their hand if they had written down that time. You can do this in five seconds intervals. When people stop raising their hands, ask if anyone has an answer longer than the last time you read out. When everyone has given their guess, then give them the correct answer. Repeat this process until you have given all of the times.

Now take the students outside to the spots that you measured. Once again have them write down how far they think it is from where they are standing to the object that you have chosen. If you changed places to measure from when you did your measuring, then it would be best to move and have them make all of their guesses before you tell them any distances. If you tell them the distance before having them guess the next one, then it will be easier for them to judge the next distance.

After they have had a chance to guess each of the distances that you measured, once again have them indicate their guess by a raise of hands as you call out various distances. After they have all indicated their guesses, then tell them the correct distance.

Both parts of this activity will show them how difficult it is to correctly judge either time or distance.

DISCUSSION IDEAS:
* How well did you do in guessing the correct time?
* Were you under or over when you guessed the time?
* How well did you do in guessing the correct distances?
* Were you under or over when you guessed the distances?
* Did you always guess under or did you always guess over? Explain.
* Would you do better or worse at this activity if you had been drinking alcohol? Explain.

- Would you do better or worse at this activity if you had been using drugs? Explain.
- How important is being able to tell distances when you are operating a car or other vehicle? Why?
- Would you want to ride in a car with someone who had been drinking alcohol? Explain.
- What are some other activities besides driving that would be hard to do if you couldn't accurately tell time or distance?

INQUIRING MINDS

TOPIC AREAS: Communication, Self-Esteem

CONCEPT: Being able to talk about yourself helps to build self-esteem. This verbalization of facts and information about your life is a reinforcement that you have worth. Some kids never have anyone actually listen to what they have to say.

METHOD: Classroom activity

TIME NEEDED: 15 minutes and discussion time

MATERIALS NEEDED:
- 1 small piece of paper (2 inches by 4 inches) for each participant
- 1 pen or pencil for each participant

ACTIVITY: Have each person write one question on a piece of paper. The question must be one that is open ended. In other words, it must not be one that can be answered "yes" or "no". The question must also ask something about the person's life rather than something trite such as, "What is your favorite food?"

Some examples of the type of questions that could be asked are:
- What class do you enjoy the most at school? Why?
- What is a trip that you took with your family?
- What was a fun Saturday that you have had recently?
- What is a favorite family tradition that you have?

- What kind of a house do you live in?
- What have you done in your life that you are proud of?
- If there was a fire in your bedroom, what would you save first?
- If you could tell your parents anything you wanted, what would it be?

As you can see this type of question gives the person answering the question a chance to describe something about the way they live, feel or think.

Once each person has written a question on their paper, you are ready to begin the activity. Have everyone find a partner. The taller of the two people will ask the shorter person the question that they have written down. The person answering the question must talk for a minimum of thirty seconds and a maximum of sixty seconds. When he/she is finished answering, then they ask the taller of the two the question that they wrote down. After both people have finished answering a question, they exchange pieces of paper and find new partners.

They will now ask the question on the piece of paper that they received in the exchange. From now on each time they find a new partner, they will exchange pieces of paper and ask someone else's question. Do not worry if the partner you chosen has already answered the question, it will be new to the person asking it. As the activity continues, each person will be asking someone else's question. This will give them quite a variety of questions to answer without having to think up more than one question.

This may sound complicated, but in practice it becomes very easy. By not having to ask a question that you created, you free the kids up from feeling so responsible for the question and they can spend their time concentrating on the answer rather than on what the other person thought of the question. If you have a really shy group, you can collect the questions from the kids before they even start. Then pass them back out to people at random. This way they won't even have to ask their own question during the first round.

If you suspect that some of the group might write down inappropriate questions, you may want to circulate around the room before starting and glance at each question to check it out. If this is a major concern for you, then circulating around the room during the question asking time will also cut down on inappropriate conversations.

This activity can be repeated a number of times during the year. It is especially good to use after school vacations or the addition of new members to your group. Some teachers have also used this process to review for a test. Then the questions center around the topic of the test rather than questions about the person.

DISCUSSION IDEAS:
- How hard was it to create a question?
- What is the difference between open and closed ended questions?
- How hard was it to answer the questions that were asked of you?
- How did you feel about asking someone else's question?

- Which question did you hear that was really interesting to you?
- How did you feel about the thirty to sixty second time limit? Too long, too short? Explain.
- What did you find out about someone that you didn't know before today?
- Do you feel that you know people, better now than before the activity? Why or why not?
- When you meet new people are these the kinds of questions you ask them? Why or why not?
- How well do you think your partner listened to you? Explain.
- What kinds of body language gave you the impression that they were interested or not?
- What are some of the ways that we can show our interest in what others have to say by our body language?
- How can this activity help us as we go through our daily lives?
- Is it important that we know about those people who are around us? Why or why not?

KANGAROO

TOPIC AREA: Diversity

CONCEPT: People come in all shapes, sizes, colors, handicaps, religions, races, etc. We need to recognize the contribution that each one can make to our school, community and society. It would be a very boring world if we were all the same. Different folks contribute different attitudes, skills religious beliefs and traditions to our communities. We need to recognize that one person is not better than another, but that each person contributes to the whole.

METHOD: Classroom activity

TIME NEEDED: 20 minutes and discussion time

MATERIALS NEEDED:
* 1 yardstick or tape measure for every two teams of five
* Masking tape

ACTIVITY: Divide your group into teams of five. Use masking tape to designate a starting line. Have the teams line up behind the starting line in single file. Explain that the object is to jump from a standing start just as far as you can. You must take off and land on two feet. Remain where you land. Have the next person on your team come up to where you landed, place their toes even with your toes and jump from there. Continue to do this until every member of your team has had a chance to jump. Have the last person stay where they landed. Use the yardstick or tape measure to measure how far your team went. Record this score with the teacher.

Take the totals from each team and figure out the average team distance on the first round. Figure out the average team distance for the second round. Put every team's totals on the blackboard. Indicate the following winning categories: The team that had the longest combined distance in round one.. The team that had the shortest combined distance in round one. The team that was closest to the first round average. Repeat the activity a second time to see how well they do on the second try.

DISCUSSION IDEAS:
- How far did your team go the first time?
- How far did your team go the second time?
- Which team had the longest distance?
- Which team had the shortest distance? Which team had the distance closest to the average on the first round?
- Which team had the distance closest to the average on the second round?
- Did everyone on your team jump the same distance? Why not?
- Did everyone contribute to the final score?
- Did the same team win each of the categories? Why not?
- How do people who have different skills contribute to our society?
- How do people that are different sizes and shapes contribute to our society?
- What would our society be like if we were all the same?

- Is it a good thing or a bad thing to have people who are different living in the same community? Why or why not?
- What can we learn from people who come from different cultures or backgrounds than ours?

KING'S X

TOPIC AREA: Advertising

CONCEPT: When you look at advertising, sometimes you really can't tell if the advertiser is telling the truth or lying to you. Half truths are really hard to distinguish. By making part of the message true, we naturally believe that the rest of the message is true. Part of being able to analyze advertising is being able to tell fact from fiction. Easy to say, but hard to do in some cases.

METHOD: Classroom activity

TIME NEEDED: 20 minutes and discussion time

MATERIALS NEEDED:
- 1 3 X 5 card for each person
- A pen or pencil for each person
- Masking tape

ACTIVITY: Give each person a 3 X 5 card. Have them print three statements about themselves; however, have only two of them be true. The third statement should be one that could be believable, but isn't true. The statements should not be about something physical such as "I have black hair". Rather the statements should be something about their past, an experience they have had, something they like or don't like, etc. This activity also allows people to get to know each other. The two truths and a lie can be written in any order on the card. Be sure to have them print clearly and large enough that others will be able to read the information on the card.

Once they have all finished writing their three statements, give each person a piece of masking tape. Have them tape the card to their right shoulder. This will allow other people to read the cards and to write on them without staring at one another's chest.

Give them five to ten minutes to wander around the room and read each other's cards. As they read each card, they are to guess which statement is the lie. Have them whisper their guess so others won't hear their answer. If they get it right, then the person whose statement they guessed puts their initials on the guesser's card. If they are wrong they must put their initials on the card of the person they guessed. The person with the most initials on their card when time is called is the winner.

DISCUSSION IDEAS:
*   How hard was it to think up two facts about yourself? Why?
*   How hard was it to think up a lie about yourself? Why?
*   How hard was it to decide which statements were true and which ones were false? Why?
*   How well did you do trying to guess?
*   How can we compare this activity to advertising?
*   Are all advertisements completely true?
*   How easy is it to be fooled by advertising?
*   What should we look for when we read an advertisement?
*   Do you think there should be a law against half truths in advertising? Why or why not?

LIAR, LIAR, PANTS ON FIRE

TOPIC AREAS: Honesty, Values

CONCEPT: Is honesty really the best policy? Do kids today know the difference between what is a lie and what is the truth? Do we still value honesty in today's society or have we replaced it with "do what is best at the time?" We talk about being honest in the family or the marriage, but what value do we really place on honesty? Here is a topic that can be addressed a lot of ways. But the bottom line is that without this vital ingredient many of the other cornerstones of our society will crumble.

METHOD: Classroom activity

TIME NEEDED: 20 minutes and discussion time

MATERIALS NEEDED:
- 1 handout of the story for each person
- 1 pencil or pen per group of four

ACTIVITY: Have your group divide into teams of about four. Hand out a copy of the story "Heather's Night Out" to each person. Designate a recorder in each group to keep track of the group ranking. Explain that after reading the story they are to rank the individuals in the story from the one who lied the most, to the one who lied the least. Most and least not meaning the most words, but the worst lie as opposed to the one telling only a "little white lie." The entire group must agree on the ranking and be ready to explain why they put them in the order they did. Share the individual group ranking with the rest of the group. Have each group explain their thinking.

Heather's Night Out

Heather and Charlotte were having a great time at the school dance. After the dance the two girls will be spending the night at Charlotte's house. When the dance ends, some friends invite them to go out for pizza. However, Heather had been told by her mother, Mrs. Hernandez, to go straight to Charlotte's after the dance. Mrs. Hernandez told Heather that she had heard some gangs might be causing trouble after the dance. She hadn't really heard this, but was concerned for Heather's safety. After all, a lot of problems do happen after dark.

Heather's mother has always been very strict when it comes to Heather. She allows her other children to do whatever they want, but not Heather. She is the only girl in a family with four boys. So Heather tells the kids she can't go out for pizza because her mother told her to go straight to Charlotte's after the dance. The group pressures her to join them saying "It's OK because you are spending the night at Charlotte's house." After a lot of arguing, Heather finally agrees with them. Heather makes Charlotte promise not to tell her mother about staying out late. When they arrive at Charlotte's house they talk for a long time and then go to sleep.

The next morning, Mrs. Hernandez arrives at Charlotte's house to pick up her daughter Heather. As the girls finish cleaning up, Mrs. Hernandez asks Heather if they had a good time at the dance. Charlotte answers quickly so Heather won't get in trouble, "We had a wonderful time and we came straight home after the dance." Charlotte doesn't like Heather's mom because she is so strict and doesn't let Heather do anything.

Charlotte's mother overhears the end of the conversation. She knows they went out for pizza after the dance, but decides it is none of her business to explain that to Heather's mother.

Later when Heather gets home she tells her mother all about the dance, sleeping over and talking all night. She doesn't mention the pizza.

Characters: Heather, Charlotte, friends, Mrs. Hernandez, Charlotte's mother.

Please rank these from the one that lied the most to the one that lied the least.

DISCUSSION IDEAS:
- How do you define the word lie?
- Do you agree with the majority of the room on who was the worst liar? Why or why not?
- Do you agree with the majority of the room on who was the least liar? Why or why not?
- Is it still lying when you know the truth but don't say it? Explain.
- Is there a difference between little lies and big lies? Describe.
- Is it OK to lie when if you told the truth it would hurt someone's feelings? Describe such a situation.
- How does lying hurt a friendship?
- How does lying hurt our society?
- Is honesty really the best policy?

- Do you know anyone who is really honest?
- How do others treat that person?
- Do you know someone who lies a lot? How do others treat that person?
- What does lying do to trust between people?

LIFEGUARD

TOPIC AREAS: Goal Setting, Support Systems

CONCEPT: Our society has made such a big deal out of people who overcome amazing odds all by themselves that we negate the importance of reaching out for help when it is needed. Relying on someone else to help us reach our goals or to help us through a tough situation has become a sign of weakness in an individual. Kids need to realize that getting help is not a sign of weakness, but rather a sign of maturity and wisdom.

METHOD: Classroom activity

TIME NEEDED: 20 minutes and discussion time

MATERIALS NEEDED:
- One pencil per team of five
- 3 metal rings from the tops of wide mouth canning jars per team
- Masking tape

ACTIVITY: Use masking tape to create two parallel lines about five to six feet apart. Adjust the distance for your group's ability. Do not make it too easy. Divide your group into teams of five. Give each team 3 metal rings and a pencil. Have one person from each team take a pencil and place it on one line, place one end on the ground and hold it in an upright position. The rest of the team takes up their position behind the other line. Have each person on the team toss the three rings and see how many of them they can get on the pencil. The holder may not move the pencil to help the ring go on it. Be sure to rotate people so everyone gets to try tossing the rings and holding the pencil. Add up the number of rings that landed on the pencil for each team. *Let them have a practice round and then a round where they keep score.*

For the next round, everything stays the same except that the person holding the pencil may move it around once the ring has been tossed. This should allow for more rings to go on the pencil. Once again be sure to rotate positions so everyone has a chance to be the tosser and the holder. Add up the number of rings that landed on the pencil for each team. *Let them have a practice round and then a round where they keep score.* Compare the scores from the first scoring round when they couldn't move the pencil and the second scoring round when they could move the pencil.

DISCUSSION IDEAS:

- How hard was it to get the ring on the pencil when it was being held still?
- How hard was it to get the ring on the pencil when it was able to be moved around?
- What made it easier when the pencil was being moved?
- When did you feel more pressure, when the pencil was stationary or moving? Why?
- How can others help us in our daily lives?
- How can others help us to reach our goals? Describe some specific situations that you have experienced.
- What kinds of people would you turn to when you needed help with a goal? With a problem?
- What are the benefits of having others help you?
- How can others help us when we are having problems?
- How can we help others when they are having problems?

LIVER FAILURE

TOPIC AREA: Alcohol

CONCEPT: Alcohol is a toxic or poison to the body. It must be eliminated from the bloodstream. This job falls to the liver. However, the liver can only process one can of beer, glass of wine or shot of hard liquor per hour. If more than this enters the bloodstream in a one hour time period, then the liver can not keep up with the detoxifying process. Also the liver has trouble processing alcohol over a period of years. The disease "cirrhosis of the liver" can be caused by overworking the liver to detoxify alcohol. This process is a slow one that occurs over a long period of time.

METHOD: Classroom demonstration

TIME NEEDED: 10 minutes and discussion time

MATERIALS NEEDED:
- 1 glass jar with a wide mouth, such as a canning jar or a quart mayonnaise jar
- 1 sponge
- A dish large enough to soak your sponge in
- 2 small, clear water glasses
- A bottle of food coloring (I use red)
- A bottle of bleach

ACTIVITY: Do this part of the demonstration without the class watching. To start, pour some bleach into the small dish. Place the sponge into the dish and allow it to become thoroughly soaked with bleach. Fill the two small glasses with water. Put a drop of food coloring in each glass so that the water turns a dark, but not real dark, shade of red. Take the sponge out of the bleach and fold it so it will fit down into the mouth of the jar. Do not push it in very far. The sponge should be covering as much of the opening as possible. You want any liquid that you pour into the jar to have to pass through the sponge on its way in. Some of the bleach will be squeezed out of the sponge and go to the bottom of the jar as you push it in the mouth of the jar . You need to get this back into the sponge. To do so, turn the jar upside down and let the sponge reabsorb the bleach. Be careful of your clothes and surfaces that you are working on. The bleach will cause damage if left on your clothes or some surfaces.

This demonstration will show how the liver detoxifies the blood by taking the alcohol out of the blood and processing it. To start the demonstration, you will take one of the glasses of water with food coloring and slowly pour it through the bleach-soaked sponge and into the jar. As the water goes through the sponge, it will become lighter in color and it should become completely clear as it reaches the bottom of the jar. Save a little of the water in the glass and compare it to the color of the water in the bottom of the jar. Explain that the sponge is playing the role of the liver and the colored water represents the alcohol in the blood stream.

Now take the other glass of colored water and pour it into the jar. Pour it in quicker than the first glass. This represents alcohol that is put into the bloodstream too quickly for the liver to process or detoxify it. You can also point out that this happens to a liver that has been working for too many years to process alcohol and has "worn out." As the water passes through the sponge, it will be darker than the first glass that you poured through. If the color is clear, then you need to pour faster. Once you have finished the demonstration, put the jar out of sight. The color will eventually disappear due to the amount of bleach that is present in the bottom of the jar. You will need to practice this demonstration a few times before you do it for your group. It takes some practice to be able to pour at the right speed and to pour so that the colored water passes slowly through the sponge. This demonstration is worth the effort. It is the closest thing I have found to show how the liver works when dealing with alcohol.

DISCUSSION IDEAS:

- How effective was the sponge when the water went through it the first time?
- How effective was the sponge when the water went through it the second time?
- How can we relate this demonstration to our own liver?
- What can this demonstration tell us about alcohol?
- What short-term problems can alcohol cause for your liver?
- What long-term problems can alcohol cause for your liver?

LIVER WORKS

TOPIC AREA: Alcohol

CONCEPT: When a person drinks alcohol it enters the bloodstream. Under normal conditions the liver takes the toxin part of the alcohol out of the bloodstream. However, when too much alcohol is introduced into the bloodstream at one time the liver cannot handle the volume. The liver starts to work overtime but if more than one beer, glass of wine or shot of hard liquor goes into the bloodstream in an hour, it cannot keep up. Some of the alcohol is passed through the liver back into the bloodstream. If this happens often enough, the liver becomes overworked and could be subjected to the disease "cirrhosis of the liver."

METHOD: Classroom activity

TIME NEEDED: 20 minutes and discussion time

MATERIALS NEEDED:
- 3 eleven inch balloons per person
- A watch with a second hand

ACTIVITY: Divide your group into teams of five. Put piles of deflated balloons around the room. They could be placed on the floor, on a chair, on a table, etc. You will need to have at least one pile of balloons per team.

Explain that your team must form a circle and put their arms around each other's waists. The object of the activity is to move as a group, without letting go of each other, from one pile of balloons to another. When you reach the pile, one team member reaches out and gets a balloon. It is then blown up and placed in the middle of the circle. It must be held in place by the stomachs of the team members. The team may only take one balloon from a pile at a time. The team must go to all of the piles before you can return to a pile a second time. If a balloon drops out of the circle, the team may stop and pick it up and put it back in the circle.

Allow the activity to go on for about ten minutes. Judge how your group is doing and change the time accordingly. You want the teams to have enough balloons that they keep dropping them on the floor. The team goal is to have the most balloons being held in their circle when time has expired. Check each group and see how many balloons they are holding when time runs out.

If you would like to repeat the activity, place the blown up balloons around the room and have them repeat the activity without having to blow up the balloons.

DISCUSSION IDEAS:
• How many balloons was your group able to hold?
• Why was your group not able to hold more balloons?
• What problems did you experience during this activity?
• How did your group overcome these problems?
• How could we compare this activity to the job your liver does?
• What happens to the alcohol in your body when the liver can't process anymore? Where does the alcohol go when the liver can't process it?

- What happens to the liver when it works too hard processing alcohol?
- What should we do to take care of our liver and keep it healthy?

LOVE AT FIRST SIGHT

TOPIC AREA: Sexuality

CONCEPT: Human sexuality is more than just the reproductive system. We need to also look at concepts such as whether men and women are treated as equals in society. We do not have this belief in many parts of the country and certainly not the world. One question that could be asked about this issue is "What kinds of occupations should males and females be encouraged to pursue?" Many cultural, social and media pressures play a role in fostering certain beliefs about this question.

METHOD: Classroom activity

TIME NEEDED: 20 minutes and discussion time

MATERIALS NEEDED:
- A handout of the characters for each student
- A pencil for each student

ACTIVITY: Explain to the class that they are going to help create a soap opera called "Love At First Sight." The action takes place in a large city hospital and has many characters. The student's job is to give a name to each of the characters. You will need to type up a handout with the list of characters on it. Break your group into teams of about three people each. They will need to agree as a team what each character will be named. They will need a first and last name for each character.

If they ask you if the character is a male or a female, just answer that the decision is up to them.

Here is a list of characters:

- A doctor who is rude to patients and thinks that they are better than everyone else
- A doctor who goes out of their way to help the homeless population of the city
- The administrator in charge of the hospital
- The secretary for the hospital administrator
- The security guard
- The janitor
- The operating room nurse
- The nurse who works in the new baby ward
- A volunteer who help the elderly patients
- A volunteer who helps in the children's ward
- The business manager of the hospital
- The drunk who comes in every Friday night to the emergency room

When the groups have completed their lists, have them give a report of the names they chose. Put a chart on the blackboard with the characters listed. As each group reads their list of names, record next to each character how many times they are given a male or a female name. At the end of the reporting time you can tally up the numbers and have an indication whether your group thinks the character is probably male or female. As I have done this exercise, it has been quite apparent that some jobs are thought of as male jobs and others as female jobs.

DISCUSSION IDEAS:

- Which jobs from this list look like they are male/ female jobs?

- What criteria did you use in your group to decide if the character was a male or a female?
- Why do we assume that some jobs are male or female?
- How has our society given us the impression that there are male and female jobs?
- Are any of the jobs that are listed definitely male or female jobs? Which ones and why?
- How does our society encourage the impression that some jobs are best filled by a certain gender?
- What can we do to change the impression that many jobs are gender related?
- At our school, does gender play a role in which programs are important and which ones aren't?
- Are the sports teams at our local schools treated the same whether they are male or female teams?
- Should male and female sports teams be treated the same?
- Should men and women be paid the same amount of money if the jobs they are doing the same?
- Should we make a list of jobs that are better filled by males or females and use that when we hire or educate people? Why or why not?

M & M MADNESS

TOPIC AREAS: Decision Making, Peer Pressure

CONCEPT: Often when decision making steps are taught, they are discussed in a vacuum. The steps are given and the students practice making a decision using the model that they have been shown. Unfortunately, in the real world more pressures and circumstances come into play than merely going through the step sequence. One of these realities is the pressure from peers. Group decision making is much harder than making a decision on your own. Just think about a situation you have been in where a group has been going out to eat and the group has to choose which restaurant they will go to. The decision can take quite a long time and not everyone is always happy with the choice. With kids it is the same way. Unfortunately many youth are drawn into destructive activities based on group decisions. Knowing how to handle the group decision making process and how to cope with group pressure is a skill our kids need to know to stay out of trouble.

METHOD: Classroom activity

TIME NEEDED: 15 minutes and discussion time

MATERIALS NEEDED:
- 1 quart size glass jar
- 1 or 2 large bags (enough to fill your glass jar) of M&M candies (I like to use the plain ones because they are harder to count)

- 1 pen or pencil per participant
- 1 piece of paper per participant

ACTIVITY: Give everyone a piece of paper and something to write with. Hold up the jar of M&M's and tell each person to guess how many are in the jar. Have them do this silently to themselves. They are not to discuss their guess with anyone. If you have the time, you can allow them to come up and take a close look at the jar. Do not let them stand there and count the candy pieces. Then have them write on their piece of paper how many candies they think are in the jar.

Now have the students get with a partner and explain that the two of them must make a guess. They must agree between the two of them what the guess will be. Have them write this second guess under the first guess. After they have all made their guesses, have the pairs join up and make groups of four. Once again the four people must agree on the number of candies in the jar. Have them write down this third guess. Have the groups of four make groups of eight and guess again. Keep repeating this process until you have joined the entire group back together into one guessing group. The second to the last guess will be a combined guess of the entire group. Now have each participant return to their seats and use the information that they gained during the discussions to make one last individual guess.

When finished, each person should have listed on their piece of paper all of the guesses that were made as they combined into larger groups in addition the first and last individual guesses. Now reveal the actual number of candies that were in the jar. Have each person circle the guess on their paper that was closest to the correct number.

DISCUSSION IDEAS:

- How many were closest when they guessed by themselves?
- How many were closest when they guessed with just one other person?
- How many were closest when they guessed with four people?
- How many people were in your group when you made the closest guess?
- In which group was it the easiest to make your decision? Explain.
- How easy was it to make your opinion known as the groups continued to get larger?
- How was it decided in each group what the correct guess would be for that round?
- What would you change about how the decision was made if we were to do this again?
- Which of your guesses was closer, your first or last individual guess?
- Did you make any change in your estimated number between your first and last individual guess? Why or why not?
- How can we relate this activity to making decision with our friends?
- Are group decisions always the best decision for every person in the group? Why or why not?
- What does each person need to do when a group decision is being made?
- What should you do if you don't agree with the decision that has been made?
- What should you do if someone else in the group doesn't agree with the decision that has been made?

The idea for this activity was suggested by Jon Wingate. Thanks, Jon!

MAGIC CARPET RIDE

TOPIC AREAS: Problem Solving, Working Together

CONCEPT: Thinking before we act and working together to solve a problem are skills that each of us need to learn. Here is a challenge that has a much better chance of being met successfully if time is taken to plan before the team acts. It also takes a great deal of cooperation to complete the task. Brainstorming, planning and working together are all skills that can be developed through this activity.

METHOD: Classroom activity

TIME NEEDED: 20 minutes and discussion time

MATERIALS NEEDED:
- One 7 foot piece of butcher paper for each team of 5 - 7 people
- 3 - 5 blindfolds for each team

ACTIVITY: Divide your group into teams of five to seven people. If your kids are large, then use the smaller group size. Give each group a piece of butcher paper about seven feet long. Find an area that is at least twenty feet long and wide enough that all of your teams can fit in it side-by-side while standing on their butcher paper. The butcher paper should be placed on the ground lengthwise with one end facing the starting line and the other end facing the finish line. This activity should take place on a carpet or tile floor. It doesn't work as well on concrete or grass. The task is easier to accomplish if the participants have their shoes off. Have this be an option they can choose, not a requirement.

Each team needs a captain. I like to use the tallest person on each team as my captains. Next, they need to figure out everyone's birthday. Part of the rules are that each time the butcher paper rips during the activity, one person becomes blindfolded. The order of blindfolding is by birthday. The person with their birthday closest to January 1 is blindfolded first and the next birthday is blindfolded second, etc. Also, if part of a person's body touches the ground off of the butcher paper, then that person becomes blindfolded. The job of the team captain is to enforce the rules, however, if he becomes blindfolded, then the next tallest person who is not blindfolded takes over as captain and enforces the rules. You won't be able to watch all of the teams, so the captain sends people to get their blindfold when a violation occurs. The blindfolds should be placed at the finish line. The team may not advance while a team member is getting the blindfold or putting it on.

The maximum number of people that can be blindfolded on a team is three on a five person team and five on a seven person team. If they reach this number and another violation occurs, then the team must sit down and either stay seated for sixty seconds. After the penalty, they may stand up and continue.

Explain that the object of the activity is to move the butcher paper from starting line to the finish line. All team members must be standing on the paper once the activity starts. You will give each team about three minutes to plan their strategy for moving the paper before they are allowed to get on the paper and start. This planning time creates a situation where they must think about what they are going to do before they do it. You may give them longer than three minutes if you want. They may not touch the paper during the planning time.

Have all teams begin at the same time with all members on the butcher paper. The activity is not over until all teams have crossed the finish line or you have declared their magic carpet destroyed and unable to complete the journey. Have the teams save their magic carpets to use during the discussion time. During the discussion, have the teams sit in their groups. This will help identify themselves when they are explaining what happened in their group.

(For your eyes only): The easiest way for them to move the paper is to have all the team members stand really close together on the end of the paper closest to the finish line. Then they reach down and carefully bunch up the paper that is behind them, leaving just enough room for them to all transfer from the end they are standing on to the other end. Then the paper is stretched out toward the finish line and the process is repeated over again. This is not the only way to accomplish this task. I have seen at least two other successful methods. Kids come up with great ideas when you let them struggle on their own.

DISCUSSION IDEAS:
* How did your group go about making its plan?
* How important was the planning time?
* Was a leader chosen in your group to help with the planning? Did the captain lead the discussion? Why or why not? How did leadership emerge?

- Was everyone's input given during the planning stage? Why or why not?
- What kinds of plans did your team come up with?
- How well did you plan work?
- What changes did you have to make when you actually started moving the paper?
- Did any team repeat the same plan over and over again even if it didn't seem to be working? Why?
- Is it OK to change a plan when you see it isn't working? Why or why not?
- How did you feel as the team captain?
- How did you feel as a follower?
- How did you feel when you were blindfolded?
- How did you feel when you were blindfolded for the paper ripping even though it might not have been your fault?
- How did you feel when you ripped the paper and someone else was blindfolded for your mistake?
- What were some of your overall feelings about this activity?
- How could you apply this activity to school?
- How could you apply this activity to the workplace?
- What would have made this activity easier?
- What would have made this activity harder?

TOPIC AREAS: Anger Management, Violence

CONCEPT: Kids react without thinking. Many arguments and fights could be avoided if people would take time to think before they acted. One of the best anger management techniques to accomplish this is to have kids take a deep breath before they respond or react to real or imagined threats to their character. This brief time-out can give them just the period they need to realize that their first reaction might cause more problems than it is worth. This is especially true if their immediate response is striking out at someone.

METHOD: Classroom activity

TIME NEEDED: 10 minutes and discussion time

MATERIALS NEEDED:
• A watch with a second hand on it

ACTIVITY: Divide your group into teams of about five. Have one person (either the teacher or an appointed designee) be the time keeper. The time keeper will keep track of the running time. They will watch each team and tell them the elapsed time when they finish. Explain that this will be a relay. The object is to see how long each team can hold their breath. You begin by counting to three. The first person on the team then takes a deep breath and holds it for as long as they can. When they need to take a second breath, the next person on the team takes a deep breath and holds it for as long as they can. Continue this process until everyone on the team has taken a turn holding their breath. When the last person on the team can't hold their breath any longer, have them signal the time keeper who will give them their elapsed time. Write the numbers down for each team. Repeat the activity to see if they can improve their time. If you have trouble with kids cheating by breathing through their nose, you may have to have them hold their nose while they are holding their breath.

DISCUSSION IDEAS:

- How easy is it to hold your breath?
- How well did your team do in the activity?
- How could holding your breath help you when you became angry?
- Some people say count to 10 when you are angry, how is holding your breath like counting to 10?
- Why would it help to count to 10 when you are angry?
- How could taking a deep breath when you are angry keep you out of trouble?
- Why is it a good idea to think before you react when you are angry?
- Describe some situations where taking some time before reacting would help keep you out of trouble.
- How does uncontrolled anger turn into violence?

OUT OF BALANCE

TOPIC AREAS: Addiction, Drugs

CONCEPT: There are many facets to each person's life. We are interested and involved in many different things that make us each a unique person. When we are well-rounded, we have a number of different areas of interest, hobbies and things we like to do. This is called leading a balanced life. When a person starts to use drugs, it can turn into an all-consuming activity. Other things that were important now seem to take a back seat. A person's drug use takes over and begins to control and dominate their life.

METHOD: Classroom activity

TIME NEEDED: 30 minutes and discussion time

MATERIALS NEEDED:
- Magazines with lots of photographs
- Scissors
- Glue
- Construction paper
- White paper
- One coat hanger for each person
- String
- Drawing materials
- Cardboard

ACTIVITY: Have each student look through magazines and cut out pictures of activities that they like to participate in. Don't just think of sports, but include eating, reading, hobbies, etc. They can also include places they would like to visit. Have them leave room around the picture when they cut it out so they can make a final cut later. Now have them glue the picture on a piece of construction paper and make the final cut. This will make the edge of the picture and the construction paper even. After they have done this, have them attach strings to the pictures and make a mobile out of it. To do this, they will tie the strings to the bottom part of a coat hanger. When finished, all of their pictures will be hanging from the bottom of the coat hanger. To help balance the mobile, they can move the photos back and forth along the bottom of the coat hanger.

Now have them draw a poster, somewhat larger than their photos, showing some kind of drug. This should be drawn on white paper and glued to the cardboard. Tie this drug poster to one end of the coat hanger. The poster should be heavy enough so that it tilts the entire mobile towards the drug picture. After the discussion time, they can remove the drug poster from their mobile. Have them draw an "X" through the drug poster and ask them to mount it on the wall next to where they hang their mobile.

DISCUSSION IDEAS:
- List the types of activities that you chose for your mobile. Why did you choose these activities?
- List the types of places that you chose for your mobile. Why did you choose these places?
- What do we mean by living a balanced life?
- What happens when we stop living a balanced life?
- How can drugs create an unbalanced life?
- Describe some of the things that we stop doing when drugs take over our life?

- What might be some of the first things to go out of our life when drugs come in?
- How can we return to a balanced life after we start using drugs?
- Who or what types of people can help us return to a balanced life?

The idea for this acitivity was suggested by Wendy Barney. Thanks, Wendy!

OVER TIME

TOPIC AREA: Peer Pressure

CONCEPT: Peer pressure is a real issue with some of our kids. We need to help them understand that the longer they are in a situation the more likely they are to give in to pressure. When an individual walks into a party and sees that it is an environment that is unhealthy and then walks out immediately, it is unlikely they will participate in any unhealthy behaviors. The chances that they will participate greatly increase the longer they stay in the unhealthy situation.

METHOD: Classroom demonstration

TIME NEEDED: 5 minutes and discussion time

MATERIALS NEEDED:
- 1 two foot length of PVC plastic pipe. You can get this at any plumbing store. Half inch to one inch works well. If they have the thin wall kind, get it.
- 3 to 4 feet of thin nylon string

ACTIVITY: Have a student come up to the front of the room and give them the string and the plastic pipe. Ask them to cut the pipe in half using just the string to do so. If they want to give it a try, go ahead and let them. Most students will just stand there or claim that they can't. At that point, have them hold the ends of the pipe firmly with two hands out in front of them. You take the nylon string and loop it around the side of the pipe that is facing away from you. In this position, only about half of the pipe is in contact with the string. Hold onto the string with both hands and start to saw back and forth in the same spot on the pipe. As you cut through the pipe, be sure that the holder doesn't pinch the string with the pipe. If they begin to pinch the pipe you will feel the string becoming harder to pull through the plastic. What you are really doing is heating up the pipe with the string. That is why you must use nylon string. It heats up the best. As you saw back and forth, the string will slowly begin cutting through the plastic pipe.

DISCUSSION IDEAS:
- What did you think when I asked him/her to cut through the pipe using only the string?
- Did you think that this was possible?
- What did you think when I began cutting the pipe?
- Were you surprised that this worked?
- How can we compare this activity to peer pressure?
- Does peer pressure always work fast? Explain.
- Is it easy to withstand peer pressure? Explain.
- Who applies the most peer pressure to you, a stranger or your best friend? Explain.
- What does this tell you about the friends that you hang around with?
- What is the best way to avoid peer pressure?
- How should you deal with a situation where you are uncomfortable?

PANDORA'S BOX

TOPIC AREA: Drugs

CONCEPT: When we talk about the effects that a certain drug will have on the body, we many times zero in on one or two effects that will be the most pronounced. For example, with tobacco it might be lung cancer or with LSD it might be hallucinations. Our kids are beginning to point to certain effects from certain drugs without realizing that there are many effects from each drug. Some effects may be more noticeable than others, but when you start putting them together they have a tremendous overall effect on the body. Also since each person reacts differently to certain drugs, we don't know for sure which effect will be most prominent in an individual.

METHOD: Classroom activity

TIME NEEDED: 20 minutes and discussion time

MATERIALS NEEDED:
- 1 quarter for each team of five
- 1 spoon for each team
- 2 tennis balls for each team
- 1 book for each team
- Masking tape

ACTIVITY: Put masking tape on the floor to designate the starting line and the turn around line. The distance between the two lines should be about fifteen feet. Divide your group into teams of five. Have them line up in single file lines behind the starting line. This activity will be run as a relay race. The round is not over until every team has completely finished. There are five rounds to the race. Have the teams stop after each round and you will give them further instructions. If someone drops an object during the race, they must return to the masking tape line they just left and start again.

Round one: Have them race with a book balanced on top of their head.

Round two: Have them race with a tennis ball between their knees.

Round three: Have them race while holding a tennis ball balanced on a spoon.

Round four: Have them race while squeezing a quarter in one of their eyes.

Round five: Have them race while doing all four actions at the same time. In this round each person will have a book on their head, a tennis ball between their knees, be holding a tennis ball in a spoon and have a quarter in one eye.

DISCUSSION IDEAS:
- How hard was it to race with the book on your head?
- How hard was it to race with the tennis ball between your knees?
- How hard was it to race with the tennis ball on the spoon?
- How hard was it to race with the quarter in your eye?

- How hard was it to race with all four things at once?
- Which one was the hardest one for you to do?
- Was this the same for each person?
- Do drugs have just one effect on our body? Explain.
- Are all effects equal on our bodies? Explain.
- Does everyone have the same effect from a drug? Why or why not?
- Can we predict what effect a drug will have on each person? Why or why not?
- What can this activity tell us about drugs and out bodies?
- What message can this activity give us about why we should avoid drug use?
- If the use of a single drug is harmful to us, what would using two or more drugs at once do to us?

PARTNERS

TOPIC AREA: Working Together

CONCEPT: Some things are just easier to do by yourself. However, sometimes you must work with others even though you think you could do the task quicker and easier by yourself. Many times this ends up to be the case when you work on a committee or in cooperative learning groups. Frustration sets in and you start to become angry with those with whom you are working. Finally you just tell them you will do it yourself and let them know when you are finished. This is especially true when more talented people are teamed up with less talented people.

METHOD: Classroom activity

TIME NEEDED: 15 minutes and discussion time

MATERIALS NEEDED: This will depend on which of the activities you wish to have them do. 1 piece of notebook paper per team of two 1 newspaper sheet and rubber band per team 1 balloon per team

ACTIVITY: Have everyone in the group get a partner. You will choose from the following activities and have them do as many of them as you would like. The key is that they must accomplish the task while holding one of their partner's hands. Task one: Make a paper airplane. Task two: Untie and tie one person's shoe. Task three: Roll up a newspaper and put a rubber band around it. Task four: Inflate a balloon and tie the end. Task five:

Both of you do a somersault at the same time, remembering that you can't let go of your partner's hand.

DISCUSSION IDEAS:
- How easy was it to do the tasks that you were given?
- What problems did you experience when completing the task?
- Would the tasks have been easier to complete if you were doing it without your partner's help? Why or why not?
- What can this activity teach us about working together?
- How hard is it to do some things as a group rather than by yourself?
- Do some people work better by themselves rather than in a group? Explain.
- Have you ever been in a situation where a group slowed you down rather than helped you?
- How frustrating is it to be slowed down?
- What are some ways when working with a group that you can keep from having problems?
- If you become frustrated when working with a group what can you do to lessen the frustration?

PICK UP STICKS

TOPIC AREAS: Decision Making, Knowledge

CONCEPT: The more information you have concerning a situation, the better decision you can make. If you already know the answer to a problem, you are way ahead of someone who is just starting to find out the answer. This can be true in the field of alcohol, tobacco and other drugs as well as such areas as sexually transmitted diseases. You don't have to experience the problems associated with these issues if you already know the consequences connected with them. Knowledge is power! We can't guarantee that the students will succeed just because of what they know, but is does give them an advantage over others.

METHOD: Classroom demonstration

TIME NEEDED: 10 minutes and discussion time

MATERIALS NEEDED:
- 15 items (these can be pencils, paper clips or even lines drawn on the blackboard)

ACTIVITY: Place the fifteen items on a table in the front of the room or draw fifteen lines on the blackboard. Ask for a volunteer to come up and play a game with you. The game goes like this. You each take turns taking one, two or three of the items during each turn. The loser is the person who has to pick up the last item. The key for you as the leader to remember is that you want to try to get items number two, six and ten. If you are able to pick these items up, especially number ten, then you will always be the winner. It doesn't matter who goes first in this game. Give your volunteer the option of going first or second to be sure that they have every opportunity to beat you.

Here is an example. Let's say that we are using fifteen pencils. The volunteer takes one pencil on their first pick. You would then take only one pencil since you are trying to be the one that takes item number two. The volunteer now takes three pencils. A total of five pencils have now been taken. Since you want to pick up item number six you would take one pencil. Let's say that the volunteer takes two pencils for a total of eight items. You would take two pencils because you are trying to get the tenth item.

Once you have the tenth item, there is no way for them to beat you. No matter what combination they use, they will lose by having to pick up the last item. Give others in the room an opportunity to challenge you. They can even get advice from the class. You may get beat once in a while by someone who lucks out and picks up the correct number of objects. If that happens simply challenge them again. For unless they know why they beat you, the chances are they won't be able to do it again. After a few rounds, explain what the secret to the game is.

DISCUSSION IDEAS:
- How hard was it to beat the teacher?
- Why was it hard to beat the teacher?
- What did the teacher know that you didn't know?
- How much of an advantage is it in a game to know something that the rest of the players don't know?

- Name some other examples where information can be an important factor in how well you do something.
- How much power does information give you?
- How can we relate information to staying away from such things as alcohol, tobacco, drugs or sexual behavior?
- Who can you gather information from that will help you keep your body healthy?
- Are there times when you get information that is incorrect? What happens then?
- How can the wrong information hurt you?
- Explain this phrase "Knowledge is power."
- How does knowledge or information give you an advantage over others?

The idea for this activity was suggested by Verne Larsen. Thanks Verne!

RAT RACE

TOPIC AREAS: Career Choices, Goal Setting

CONCEPT: What do you want to be when you grow up? This question is asked a million times to every kid as they go through school. It may be disguised in different terms, but it is still the same question parents and teachers have been asking since the start of the industrial revolution. With so many occupations now available and training becoming more and more specialized for certain occupations, an early choice of careers can be helpful. More important than that, a career choice can help motivate youth to set goals and work towards their goals rather than engaging in harmful behavior that would circumvent them from reaching those goals.

The choice of a job is also important because of the time that you will spend doing it each day. Most people spend more time on their job than any other activity during a week. Much of your satisfaction in life will come from how much you enjoy your job.

METHOD: Classroom activity

TIME NEEDED: 30 minutes and discussion time

MATERIALS NEEDED:
- 1 set of newspaper classified ads, employment section, for every two people (The classified ads do not have to be identical for each pair)
- Writing paper, pencil or pen for each pair

ACTIVITY: Have everyone choose a partner. Give each pair a pen or pencil, one piece of writing paper and a set of classified ads, which show the employment opportunities, from the newspaper. Explain that each of them are to select three jobs from the paper which they think would be interesting jobs.

After they select the three jobs, have them discuss with each other the following discussion questions relating to those jobs. This will give them a chance to verbalize their career interests and to describe those interests to someone else.

DISCUSSION QUESTIONS:
- What kind of education would you need to have to be hired for this job?
- Does this job pay a low wage, an average wage or a high wage?
- Why would this job be enjoyable?
- What part of this job would be not so enjoyable?
- What would be the hardest part of this job?
- Is this the kind of job you could do for the rest of your life? Why or why not?

Once they have finished discussing these questions for their three selections with each other, have them each decide on one of their selections that they will share with the entire group. When they present their job selection, have them use the discussion questions as an outline.

DISCUSSION IDEAS:
- How easy was it to select a job? Explain.
- What were you looking for when you were deciding on a job selection?

- What makes one job a good one and another job a bad one?
- How important is it to get a job that you enjoy doing?
- What happens if you get a job and hate going to work everyday?
- What role does education play in the choice you have of a job?
- Are some jobs more important than others? Why or why not?
- How can knowing your career choice help you in setting goals for yourself?
- How can using alcohol, tobacco or other drugs hurt your chances of getting the job that you want?
- How can behaviors such as sexual activity or gang membership hurt your chances of getting the job that you want?
- How can other people help you decide what career would be a good one for you?
- How can other people help you reach your career goals?
- Should other people choose your career for you? Why or why not?
- Once you have chosen a career, what can you do if you end up not liking it?

RIGHT CHOICE

TOPIC AREA: Refusal Skills

CONCEPT: When teaching kids how to say "No", we have to take into account that how we say "No" might depend on the situation we are in. We wouldn't take the same approach with our best friend as we would with a stranger at a party. By giving your students more than one way to say "No", you are helping them with the realities of the real world. By thinking about various ways to say "No" ahead of time, they will be better prepared when faced with the situation.

METHOD: Classroom activity

TIME NEEDED: 10 minutes and discussion time

MATERIALS NEEDED: None

ACTIVITY: Have your group stand in a circle. Choose one person to be in the middle. Explain that the game is played just like the traditional "Rocks, Paper and Scissors" game except that everyone in the circle is playing against the person in the middle. Remember that a rock is represented by a clenched fist, paper is represented by the open palm and scissors are represented by having two fingers showing like the blades of a pair of scissors. A rock breaks scissors, paper covers rock and scissors cut paper. Have everyone in the circle turn around and face out of the circle. Count "one, two, three, go!" At the word go everyone in the circle turns and does one of the three hand signals. The person in the middle also chooses one of the three hand signals. Everyone in the circle checks to see how they did against the person in the middle. Play a few rounds just to get the feel of the game. Each round or two, change the person in the middle by choosing someone at random to replace them.

For the second part of the activity change the rules slightly. If you are beaten by the person in the middle, you have to sit down or step back out of the circle. If you have the same hand sign as the person in the middle, nothing happens. Play a few rounds until most people are sitting. Continue to change the person in the middle after each round or two by randomly choosing someone who is still left standing. You may repeat this part of the activity as many times as you wish. Just let everyone back in to play again.

Repeat the activity with one more change. Get everyone back into the circle, except for one person in the middle. This time have the person in the middle announce what hand motion they are going to do before you start counting. You will probably only have to do this part of the activity once to get the message across that if you know what they are going to do, then your own choice will be easy.

VARIATION: If lack of time or space is an issue, this game may also be played with the leader in front of the group. The group does not have to be in a circle, they may simply be facing the leader. I still like to have them turn around when you are counting. This adds more movement to the activity. However, you may just have them face the leader if you want.

DISCUSSION IDEAS:

- How well did you do against the person in the middle?
- Did you always use the same hand signal for each round? Why or why not?
- Which person in the game was it the best to be, the person in the circle or the person in the middle? Why?
- How hard was the game when you knew what the person in the middle was going to do?
- Do different situations where you are being pressured to use drugs require different types of responses?
- What would happen if you used the same response in all situations?
- How would you tell your best friend "No"?
- How would you tell a close friend "No"?
- How would you tell someone you sort of knew "No"?
- How would you tell a stranger "No"?
- Does it really matter how well you know the person?
- Would the situation you are in determine how you said "No"?
- Give some examples. If you knew in advance what the situation might be and planned ahead, would it be easier to say "No"?
- Who has the upper hand in the conversation, the person applying the pressure or the person having the pressure applied to them? Explain.

RIVER OF FIRE

TOPIC AREAS: Problem Solving, Working Together

CONCEPT: Being able to work as part of a team to solve problems is one of the employee characteristics that our large and small companies alike are screaming for. The challenges in today's workplace call for combining knowledge with common sense in an effort to increase productivity. Workers who lack the ability to look at a problem from more than one angle or who are locked into simply following someone else's instructions are not going to advance. We need to allow our students opportunities to experience solving problems that have no easy or right solution.

METHOD: Classroom activity

TIME NEEDED: 40 minutes and discussion time

MATERIALS NEEDED:
- Twenty feet of thin rope for each team of 4-6
- 3 tennis balls per team
- 4 blindfolds per team
- 1 roll of masking tape

ACTIVITY: This activity is set up by using masking tape to create the edges of the river. The lines need to be set ten feet apart. If you have multiple teams, you can either make a number of river all around the room or just make one long river and space them out along it. On one side of the river you place two blindfolds and the rope. On the other side you place two blindfolds and three tennis balls. Divide your group into teams of four to six people. Have them sit in their groups and read the following story to them.

YOUR SPECIAL MISSION

An environmental team has been sent to an island to dispose of three radioactive containers. The team's helicopter has crash landed next to a molten lava river that no one can get across. Part of the team has landed on one side of the river and the rest of the team landed on the other side. All three containers landed on one side of the river. Everything burned during the crash except for four pieces of cloth, a length of rope and the clothes that you are wearing. The radioactive containers are emitting a radioactive light that can't be seen, but is deadly to the human eye. Therefore, anytime anyone touches the containers or the rope, he/she must be blindfolded.

Your job is to transport the three containers from one side of the river to the other so they can be moved to a safer location. The containers must not be subjected to quick movements or they will explode. Since the containers might explode, they must be moved across the river one at a time. Nothing can be used from the surrounding area to help you transport the containers because the area is infected with a jungle virus that is spread by touching. If during the transporting of the containers any part of the rope, the containers or the bodies of the team members touch the river, then all three containers must be returned (by the river guardian) to the side of the river from which they came.

Good Luck and Be Safe!

After you read the story to the students, allow three minutes of planning time for each team to discuss strategies among themselves. At the end of the planning time, they must divide themselves up on the two sides of the river with whatever number on each side they feel will work best and begin to move the containers. Once the division is made, they must remain on that side of the river. They may still talk as they work on the problem. As the river guardian, you are protected from the heat of the river and can freely move back and forth across the river.

Be sure to watch to make sure they obey the restriction that anyone who touches the rope or containers is blindfolded. If you would like, you may place a time limit on how long they have to accomplish this task. Calling out the time left in the activity can help create tension. If you see them ready to swing, fling or throw the containers across, remind them that quick movements will cause the containers to explode. If any of these restrictions make the activity too hard or too easy for your group, simply make changes to accommodate the abilities of your group.

Solution ideas: They will be able to just throw the rope across. The hard part will be doing it blindfolded. Figuring out the containers is a little harder. One solution is to use the blindfolds to transport the containers across the river. They can tie a tennis ball up in a blindfold. Then they tie the blindfold around the rope and slide it across the river. If you wish to make the activity harder, eliminate this as an option or allow it to be used for the first container only. Other possible solutions include using a shoe, shirt or other article of clothing to transport the containers across the river using the rope. To accomplish this, one person holds the rope up high on one side of the river and another person holds it done low on the other side of the river. Then you tie whatever you are using (for example, a shoe) to transport the containers over the rope and use it as a "zip line" to slide items across the river. There are other solutions; let the kids show them to you.

DISCUSSION IDEAS:
- What was your first reaction to the activity?
- What did your team do during the planning time before the activity started?
- How were the plans made? Was your original plan successful?
- What changes did you have to make during the activity?
- Who was your leader during the activity? How was this person chosen? Did the leader change during the activity? Why or why not?
- Which person would you rather be: the leader or follower? Why?
- Was your team successful in completing the assignment?
- If you were to do this activity again, what would you do differently? Why?
- How many people did you put on each side? Why? Would you do it differently next time?
- What can we learn from this activity?
- Where in our daily lives can you apply the lessons you learned during this activity?
- How does this activity compare with being in the workplace?

SAY IT AND DO IT

TOPIC AREA: Values

CONCEPT: When we really believe in something, it is difficult for us to behave in a manner that is not consistent with what we believe. Take honesty for example. If you firmly believe that honesty is the best policy and a classmate asks you to share your answers with him on the test that day, your answer will be an automatic "no." If for some reason you do end up getting talked into sharing answers, then you will feel badly about the incident and either never repeat the behavior or you will change your values. You may adopt the value that cheating is only OK when it is helping a good friend or some other rationalization. Your values are reflected in your behavior.

METHOD: Classroom activity

TIME NEEDED: 10 minutes and discussion time

MATERIALS NEEDED: None

ACTIVITY: Have the entire group stand up and face you. Explain that you will point both of your arms in one direction and they are to copy you by pointing both of their arms in the same direction and to call out the direction that they are pointing. You can only do four directions. You can raise your arms over your head, point them down towards your feet or point them to the left or to the right. Go through these four directions and have the students copy you and call out the direction

that they are pointing. Be sure they understand that
the directions are how they see them. This means that
you will be pointing your arms to your left, but for them
it is their right. When they call out the direction they
are to use their own right and left.

After letting them practice, it is time for the real
thing. Move your arms to one of these four positions and
wait for them to move their arms and to call out the
direction. Repeat this process a number of times, moving your arms to a different one of the four positions
each time.

Stop and explain that you are changing the assignment. This time you want them to move their arms the
same direction that you do but say the opposite direction. For example, you move your arms down. They
would move their arms down, but they would say "Up."

For the third round, they are to say the direction
that your arms move, but they are to move their arms
in the opposite direction. For example, you put your
arms over your head. They should say "Up" but move
their arms down. I can guarantee that this process
becomes quite confusing.

Now that they have all had the experience start over
again. This time if they make a mistake, they have to
sit down. Continue just as before. Start by repeating the
same sequence and see how many of them remain after
each change. The pressure of having a consequence for
making a mistake more closely relates the pressure of
how our values effect our behavior. Encourage those
that make a mistake to help you watch for those who
make an incorrect movement or call out an inappropriate direction.

DISCUSSION IDEAS:

- How hard was it to move your hands and call out the same direction that I was doing?
- How hard was it to say the correct direction and move your hands in the opposite direction?
- How hard was it to say the opposite direction and move your hands in the correct direction?
- Why was this hard to do?
- How did the change make you feel when we added the rule about being out if you made a mistake? Did you feel any added pressure?
- How hard is it for you to say one thing but to be thinking another?
- How hard is it to act one way when you are feeling another way?
- Describe a situation where someone has acted in a manner differently from the way they think or feel?
- How important does this make your values?
- Can we act differently from what we really believe? Explain.
- How do our values or beliefs dictate what our behavior will be?

TOPIC AREA: Communication

CONCEPT: When we have clear communication not only are problems a lot easier to solve, but in some cases they don't come up at all. Young people need to see how communication can help them in their daily lives.

METHOD: Classroom activity

TIME NEEDED: 15 minutes and discussion time

MATERIALS NEEDED: None

ACTIVITY: Everyone will need a partner for this activity. Explain that the action of the game is a lot like the game called "Paper, Rocks and Scissors". At least the part about counting to three and throwing your fingers out is a lot like that game. Nothing else about it is. You will give them sixty seconds to see how many times the two of them can throw their fingers out and come up with the number seven between them. They may not discuss ahead of time how they will accomplish this.

Have them count to three and then extend a number of fingers on one hand. Each person will have a certain number of fingers showing. Between the two people the object is to have exactly seven fingers showing. Have them keep trying and see how many times they can get exactly seven during the sixty seconds. When the time is up, ask the various partners how many times they were able to get exactly seven.

Now have them get in teams of three. The same rules apply except that they are trying to get the number eleven. At the end of sixty seconds, ask how they did on this one. Now have them try it again in teams of five while trying to get the number 21. Once again, check the results.

For the last round have them get into teams of seven. This time they will be going for the number 30. Before they start, give them thirty seconds to talk about how many fingers each person should throw so they add up to 30.

DISCUSSION IDEAS:
- How hard was it to throw a seven?
- How hard was it to throw an eleven?
- How hard was it to throw a twenty-one?
- How hard was it to throw a thirty?
- What made the throwing of the thirty easier than the other numbers?
- What do you think the object of this activity is?
- Why is clear communication so important?
- What happens when we do not have clear communication?
- Describe a situation where unclear communication caused you or a friend a problem.
- What are some steps we can take to be sure that we communicate clearly?

SHRINKING STRAW

TOPIC AREA: Tobacco

CONCEPT: Tobacco effects various parts of the body. Two of these are the lungs and the blood vessels. Tar builds up in the lungs, causes damage to alveoli which results in a decreasing capacity to breath. As more and more alveoli become damaged, the lungs have less and less usable space to breath. The result is a shortness of breath and a corresponding quickening of the breathing pattern. A second effect is the constricting of the arteries or blood vessels. Nicotine is the culprit here. As the blood vessels constrict, the heart must pump harder and faster to maintain the same amount of blood flow to the various body parts. This increased work load is a contributing factor to heart failure.

METHOD: Classroom activity

TIME NEEDED: 20 minutes and discussion time

MATERIALS NEEDED:
- Kool Aid, punch or some other beverage
- 1 regular drinking straw for each participant
- 1 cocktail drinking straw (the real thin ones) for each participant
- 1 small paper cup for each participant with a few extras
- A watch with a second hand

ACTIVITY: Divide your group into teams of about five. Place one cup per participant on a table and fill them with Kool Aid. If the cups are too large for them to drink three of them, then only fill the cups half full. Each participant should be given a regular drinking straw. Explain that this is a relay. Have the team gather around their cups. One person on the team will put their straw in their cup of Kool Aid and drink until it is gone. They do not have to drink it all without taking a breath. Have them remember which paper cup was the one they used or write their names on them. Repeat this process until all the team members have had a turn. Keep track of how long it takes for the entire team to be finished. Record each team's result. Now fill back up the cups and repeat the process again to see if they can beat their first round times.

For the third round fill the cups up again but exchange everyone's regular drinking straw for one of the thin cocktail drinking straws. Once again have everyone on each team take turns emptying their cups and compare the timed results with the first two rounds.

DISCUSSION IDEAS:
- How did you do in the first round?
- Did your team get better in the second round? Why?
- How did you do in the third round with the smaller straw? How did the results of the third round compare with the results of the first two rounds?
- What was the difference between the first two rounds and the third round?
- How can we compare this activity to the effects of tobacco on the body?
- What happened when the straw became narrower? How does this compare with the blood vessels of a smoker?

- Was it harder to suck through the smaller straw? How does this compare with the lungs of a smoker?
- What activities in your life would be harder to do if your body was effected by smoking?
- What types of jobs would be hard for you to have if you were a smoker?

SLOW LEAK

TOPIC AREAS: Addiction, Drugs

CONCEPT: We should not lie to our students and tell them that drugs do not sometimes give their bodies a good feeling. To do this would make everything else we say suspect. Under most conditions, drugs do produce a pleasurable feeling. If this was not true, then we would not have the widespread use of drugs that we have today. You don't see people rushing out to use "Clorox"!

However, just because we can receive a good feeling from drugs, that does not mean we should downplay the harmful effects that can go along with that perceived good feeling. One issue that should be shared with our students is the fact that this feeling does not last. Some drugs have a very short life, while effects of others may last longer. The fact remains that the "high" feeling from all drugs will wear off sooner or later. This plays a roll in addiction. If your body or mind begins to crave the effect of the drug, then you will become addicted to it. Another factor is the "coming down or off" a drug. As the effect wears off, you don't go back to feeling normal; you actually feel worse than before you took the drug. With this depressed or physically painful feeling, many drug users want to get some more of the drug into their system as soon as possible.

METHOD: Classroom activity

TIME NEEDED: 15 minutes and discussion time

MATERIALS NEEDED:

* One balloon per person, plus a few extras (These should all be the same size and shape. I like to use 9 inch round balloons.)
* Masking tape

ACTIVITY: Divide your group into teams of five. If you have an odd number, have some people repeat the course to make the teams even. Find an area that is about fifteen feet long and wide enough for all of your teams to stand single file, side-by-side. Use the masking tape to put two lines on the floor. One for the starting line and another line about fifteen feet from the start. The tape should be long enough to go across in front of all of your teams.

Explain that you are going to give each person a balloon. The object is for them to blow up the balloon while standing behind the starting line. If they can't blow the balloon up, a team member may blow it up for them. Tell them to leave the end of the balloon untied. Then when it is their turn to walk, they are to walk as far as they can with the balloon in their hand. They may not hold onto the end of the balloon to slow down the escaping air. They must hold it either on the sides or the end opposite the opening. When the balloon runs out of air, they stop right where they are. If they reach the masking tape line before the air stops coming out of their balloon, then they turn around and head back to the starting line.

This is a relay race. Therefore, the next person in line will start wherever the person before them ran out of air. They are to have their balloon already blown up, and then walk out to the spot where the previous team member ran out of air and start from there. They must head in the same direction that their team mate was heading when the balloon ran out of air. The person whose balloon had run out of air goes back and joins the rest of the his/her team behind the starting line. Each team needs to keep track of how many times they went up and back during the race. Each direction counts as one point. Remember: no running, only walking. Repeat the activity a couple of times to see if they got better the second time around.

DISCUSSION IDEAS:
- How many steps did you take before your balloon ran out of air?
- Did you feel that the air ran out of the balloon fast or slow?
- Were some people able to travel farther than others? Why or why not?
- What effected how far you were able to travel?
- How well were you able to control how long the air stayed in your balloon?
- How can the balloons relate to the length of time drugs stay in your body?
- Can we control the length of time a drug stays in our body?
- Do some drugs last longer in your body than others? Which ones?
- Do any drugs last forever in your body?
- What happens to your body after the good feeling of some drugs goes away?
- How can this painful feeling after using drugs cause a person to become addicted to the drug?

SOMEONE MISSED

TOPIC AREA: Stress

CONCEPT: We can handle problems that come at us one at a time. Our stress usually results when problems come at us too fast for us to handle. Normally there is not one big stressor that wipes us out, but a number of small ones that by themselves would not be a problem, but when combined drive us to such behaviors as alcohol or other drug use, depression or violence.

METHOD: Classroom activity

TIME NEEDED: 15 minutes and discussion time

MATERIALS NEEDED:
- 1 tennis ball for every two people

ACTIVITY: Everyone stays together in a group for this activity. Have everyone stand in a loose bunch. You start with one tennis ball. Someone throws it up and someone else has to catch it. The ball must travel at least ten feet into the air and no more than fifteen feet into the air. The person that catches it then throws it up and another person catches it. No one may catch the ball twice. Names may not be called out as to who is supposed to catch the ball. Continue the activity until everyone has had a chance to catch the ball. Count the number of times that the ball hits the ground.

For the second round start the same way. Have one person throw one tennis ball in the air and someone else must catch it. If the ball is caught then you add another ball. Give this ball to someone different. Now two balls will be thrown in the air and caught by someone other than the person who threw the ball. Anyone can catch the ball, except the person who threw it, even if they have already caught one previously. Once again, names may not be called out as to who is to catch the balls. Each time the balls are thrown and caught, add another ball to the activity. Keep track of how many balls the group can catch before one is dropped.

DISCUSSION IDEAS:
- How hard was the first part of the activity when we were throwing just one ball?
- How difficult was the second part of the activity when there was just one ball?
- How difficult was it as you added more and more balls?
- How much pressure did you feel to be sure that you were not the one to drop the ball?
- How can this activity be related to stress in our lives?
- What are some of the day-to-day stressors that we live with?
- Are any of these by themselves enough to really stress us out?
- What happens when we have a lot of little stressors?
- What are some things we can do to reduce our stress?
- How can others help us with our stress?
- If we use alcohol or other drugs to reduce our stress what are some of the negative consequences?
- Can stress produce feelings such as anger?
- What can we do when we feel angry due to stress?

SOME CALL IT ART?

TOPIC AREA: Communication

CONCEPT: Verbal communication consists of two parts. One part is talking and the other is listening. Both are equally important even though we usually want to talk more than we want to listen. We can understand a difficult concept or detailed information better when we have someone to help us. Once we understand the importance of listening to others, we will be more apt to utilize information from those who can help us rather than only using the information that we ourselves have. Clear message sending and active listening play important roles in clear communication.

METHOD: Classroom activity

TIME NEEDED: 25 minutes and discussion time

MATERIALS NEEDED:
- 2 pieces of paper per person
- 1 pen or pencil per person
- 3 drawings that you have created as the sample pictures

ACTIVITY: Everyone will need a piece of paper and something to draw with. You will need to create a picture for them to recreate. Don't worry it will not have to be a work of art. You will just want the basic outlines of various objects in the picture. Hold the picture up in front of the group. Let them look at it for about twenty seconds. Now tell them to close their eyes and draw the same picture on their piece of paper. Don't make the picture too hard, but have enough detail that they have to move their pencil around the paper and try to line up things in the picture. For this drawing I usually use a house with a door, chimney, smoke, a couple of windows, a mailbox to one side and a tree on the other side. Allow two minutes or so for them to draw the picture. After they have completed their drawings hold up your picture and have them compare their results with the original picture.

For round two you will need a new picture. You may use a different version of a house or you may choose a new subject to have them draw. This time have them get into pairs. The person drawing will need a piece of paper and a pencil. Have the person drawing close their eyes. They will have to draw the picture with their eyes closed while their partner tells them what to draw.

Now hold up the new picture. Their partner will be able to see the picture and can guide them while they draw. They may not touch the person who is doing the drawing, but they may verbally direct them as to where to put their pencil and how long to draw each line. Give them about four minutes to complete this round.

For round three, have the partners switch roles and repeat the activity. You will want to use a new picture since the person drawing will have already seen the one you have just used. At the conclusion of rounds two and three, once again hold up your sample picture so they can see how well they have done.

DISCUSSION IDEAS:
- How well did you do drawing the first picture by yourself?

- What made it hard to draw the first picture?
- How well did you do drawing the picture with your eyes closed when someone was helping you?
- Was it difficult or easy to follow the other person's directions? Why?
- How easy was it to give the directions to your partner for them to draw? What made it hard or easy?
- How well did your partner follow your directions?
- Were the pictures more or less accurate when you had someone helping you than when you did one yourself? Explain.
- What can this activity tell us about communication?
- How easy is it to explain something to someone else?
- How easy is it to understand what others tell us?
- Describe a situation where getting the exact directions would be very important.
- Have you ever heard of a situation where communication has not been clear and a misunderstanding resulted?
- Have any of your friends gotten mad because of something they thought they heard and later it turned out the person really didn't say that? Describe.
- Why is clear communication important?
- What kinds of problems does confusing communication create?
- What can we do to make sure our communication is clear?

SOUNDS LIKE

TOPIC AREA: Communication

CONCEPT: In the communication process, the area of active listening has had a lot of emphasis. All of the "I Messages" in the world will not do any good if no one listens to what you have to say. Active listening begins with the premise that you are actually hearing what the other person has to say. This kind of listening is more than just hearing the words that are spoken. This kind of listening requires the recipient of the communication to not only listen, but concentrate on what is being said rather than just waiting for their turn to talk.

METHOD: Classroom activity

TIME NEEDED: 20 minutes and discussion time

MATERIALS NEEDED:
- Tape recorder
- Audio tape with sounds that you have prerecorded
- Paper and pencil for each team of two or three

ACTIVITY: Before the activity, you will need to tape record various sounds. You will need to record nine to fifteen different sounds. The easiest way to do this is to make a list of sounds that you want to record and record them in that order. This eliminates the need to transfer the sounds to another tape to put them in the order that you want to play them.

Each sound needs to be recorded twice, with a period of silence between each recording. This period of silence will give you a chance to stop the tape recorder. These can be simple sounds such as a car horn honking or they can be more difficult such as a garbage disposal. The sounds chosen should be age appropriate for your group. Don't make them too easy. Have some that are really hard. The game will be played in three rounds. The sounds for each round should get progressively harder to identify. Some of the sound I have used are a typewriter, car horn, alarm clock, popcorn popping, washing machine agitating, toilet flushing, someone eating a corn chip, sewing machine, telephone ringing, and a pencil sharpener. You are only limited by your own imagination.

Start the activity by dividing your group into teams of two or three. Each team will need one piece of paper and a pencil. Explain that you will be playing a tape recording of certain sounds. Each sound will be repeated twice. Play the sound the first time and then give the teams a few seconds to discuss what they think it is. Now play the sound a second time and have them write down their answer. Repeat this process for all of the sounds that you have recorded.

Break the activity into three rounds. Explain that round one (the first third of the sounds) is worth one thousand points for each correct answer, that round two (the second third of the sounds) is worth two thousand points for each correct answer and that round three (the last third of the sounds) is worth three thousand points for each correct answer. Stop after you have completed each round. Give the correct answers after each round and let the groups see how they are doing.

DISCUSSION IDEAS:

- How easy was it to identify the sounds that you heard?
- Did you usually identify the sound the first time it was played or the second time. What helped you to identify each sound?
- Which sounds were the easiest for you to identify?
- Which sounds were the hardest for you to identify?
- Did you listen harder to the one thousand point sounds or the three thousand point sounds? Why or why not?
- How can this activity be compared to communication?
- What does listening have to do with communication?
- How hard do we listen to others?
- Why is it important to listen to others?
- How can poor listening lead to arguments and fights?
- What kinds of things get in the way of listening to what others have to say?
- What can we do to make ourselves better listeners?
- What types of body language do we use when we are really listening hard to someone?
- When someone listens to you, how does that make you feel?
- How does it make you feel when you aren't listened to?

SPIDERMAN

TOPIC AREAS: Depression, Self-Esteem, Suicide

CONCEPT: As we go through life people say things and events happen that affect us emotionally. It may be as simple as someone telling us our hair looks funny or as devastating as the loss of someone we loved. We are not going to get people to stop making sarcastic or hurtful remarks, and we are not going to be able to have a great deal of impact on events that surround us. Instead we must take a look at how we respond to what is said and to what happens. If we allow others to adversely affect our thinking, then our emotional state will always be at the mercy of others. A continual pattern of this kind of emotional manipulation can result in individuals being drawn into a downward cycle that affects not only their self-esteem, but eventually their entire emotional well being.

METHOD: Classroom activity

TIME NEEDED: 25 minutes and discussion time

MATERIALS NEEDED:
- 4 pieces of paper the size of one quarter of a piece of notebook paper per person
- 1 pen or pencil per person
- Masking tape
- A watch with a second hand

ACTIVITY: Give each person four pieces of paper. On each of the four sheets of paper, have them write one thing that people might say that make other people feel badly. They are to write four different statements, one per piece of paper. These do not have to be things that people have said directly to them or even about them, just generic things that are said which make people feel bad. Some suggestions would be "Your hair is really ugly today." "That outfit makes you look like a . . . " "You aren't going out with him/her are you?" " You're so dumb." After everyone has finished writing their statements, collect them and read them aloud to the group.

Now divide your group into teams of four or five. Use masking tape to make a line about twelve to fifteen feet away from a wall. If you don't have access to a wall, you can mark the distance with more masking tape. Have the teams line up single file behind the masking tape. The teams should be facing the wall. For the first round, the teams are to walk, normal speed, in relay fashion from the starting line to the wall and back. Use the watch to read out the times as the teams finish. Keep track of each team's finishing time.

For round two, pass out one of the pieces of paper that the kids wrote on to each person. They will not purposely receive their own paper. If it happens to be handed to them, don't worry, it doesn't effect the activity. Explain that for this round they will once again walk up to the wall and back relay style, but they will have to put the piece of paper under one foot and drag it along with them as they walk. When they reach the wall, have them reach down and pick up the paper and carry it back to the starting line in their hand. Tell them not to discard the paper when they have finished. It will be used again later in the activity. Once again keep track of each team's finishing time and compare it to the first round's time.

For round three once again pass out another piece of paper with a statement on it. This time they will have to walk up to the wall with two pieces of paper, the one from the first round and the one you just handed them, one under each foot. Then they will carry the papers back to the starting line in their hands. Record their times and compare with the previous round.

For rounds four and five continue to give them another piece of paper for each round. They will have to slide these pieces of paper along the floor with their hands in addition to sliding their other papers under their feet. On the return trip back to their team, they will carry all of the papers in their hands back to the starting line with them. For round four they will have a piece of paper under each foot and one under a hand. Then for round five they will have papers under both feet and both hands. Record their times and compare each round with the previous ones.

DISCUSSION IDEAS:
- How hard was the first round?
- How hard was each successive round?
- What happened to the times for each team as we kept adding pieces of paper?
- How can this activity be compared to what happens to people in their lives?
- What are some of the other ways that people lose self-esteem and become depressed?
- Can we control what others say or do? Explain.
- Can we control how we react to what others say and do? Explain.
- What happens to us if we let what others say and do affect how we feel?
- How can this process lead to suicide?

- How do people act when they are depressed?
- How does feeling down affect our own actions? What can we do to not allow others to impact how we feel?
- How can we get out of a depressed mood?
- How can others help us get out of a depressed mood?
- How can we help others not become or stay depressed?
- How do the people we hang around with affect our moods and images of ourselves?

The idea for this activity was suggested by Jeanine Carter. Thanks Jeanine!

STICK IT

TOPIC AREAS: Anger Management, Communication

CONCEPT: Miscommunication causes problems. Clearly expressing what we want someone else to do will help them respond appropriately. Without clear information that allows others to accomplish what we want, frustration on the part of both the person giving information and those receiving the information may occur. This frustration may quickly turn into anger.

METHOD: Classroom activity

TIME NEEDED: 10 minutes and discussion time

MATERIALS NEEDED:
- A pen or pencil for each person
- A piece of paper about 2 X 2 inches for each person
- A 2 inch piece of masking tape for each person
- Wall space where the teacher can hang a 2 feet by 3 feet blank sheet of paper

ACTIVITY: Before the activity starts and before the students are watching you, hang a sheet of paper on the wall. The paper should be about 2 feet by 3 feet in size. Hang it where the students can get to it. Each person will need something to write with, a small piece of paper and a short piece of masking tape. Have them write their name on the piece of paper. When everyone is finished explain that you want them to place their piece of paper with their name on it somewhere in the room using the masking tape. When they have placed their name they are to return to their seats. Do not give anymore instruction than this.

When everyone is seated, begin to scold them for placing their names in the wrong place. You did not want them to be placed where they are, what you wanted was for all of the names to be placed on the sheet of paper that you hung on the wall. Emphasize that they should be better listeners and they should cooperate when you give them an instruction. After you have spent some time telling them how disappointed you are that they couldn't do what you wanted them to, stop and point out that you realize that it is hard to do something right when we aren't given complete information. You realize that they aren't mind readers.

However, to prove how much better they could do if given the right information you are going to give them another task. Have them walk over and stand by their piece of paper. Now explain that you want them to close their eyes and move their piece of paper from where it is to the sheet of paper that you have on the wall. They are to complete the task with their eyes closed. Once they have placed their paper on the sheet on the wall, they may open their eyes and return to their seats. You will find that even with the obstacle of having their eyes closed, most of them will be able to accomplish the task now that they know what it is you really want them to do.

DISCUSSION IDEAS:
* What was your reaction when I asked you to place the paper somewhere in the room?
* How hard was it to decide where to put your piece of paper?

- What were your thoughts when I was unhappy with you for not putting your paper where I wanted it?
- How hard was it to put your paper in the proper place, even with your eyes closed?
- Have you ever had someone give you information that wasn't complete?
- What did you do in that situation?
- Is it harder or easier to do something when you have all of the information? Why or why not?
- What could you do to make sure that you receive all of the information?
- What can you do to make sure that someone does what you want?
- How do you feel when an important part of the information gets left out?
- What is an action that you might take when you get frustrated that would cause you more problems?
- How can you get rid of a negative feeling that is due to a communication problem, in a positive manner?

STICKS AND STONES

TOPIC AREAS: Self-Esteem, Violence

CONCEPT: "Sticks and stones may break my bones, but words will never hurt me!" This age old saying has never been true and with today's kids it may lead to more than hurt feelings. One of the factors in lowering self-esteem and the outbreak of violence are the words that we use. We need to help our kids realize that their words, tone of voice and body language all have an effect on what others hear us say. The same words can be used in different situations and provoke different reactions. You can call a friend a name and both end up laughing. Call someone else that same name and they may want to fight.

METHOD: Classroom demonstration

TIME NEEDED: 5 minutes and discussion time

MATERIALS NEEDED:
- Hammer
- Nail Board
- Empty aluminum soda pop can

ACTIVITY: In front of the class, take the hammer and pound the nail into a piece of wood. Explain that this is one way to use a hammer. Now take the same hammer and smash the empty aluminum soda pop can. Explain that this is also a way to use a hammer but it produces a much different outcome.

DISCUSSION IDEAS:

- Was the hammer made to drive nails?
- Was the hammer made to change the shape of things?
- In both cases, is it the same hammer?
- How many ways can a hammer be used? List some.
- Can you expect a different outcome when you use a hammer in different ways? Explain.
- How can words be compared to a hammer?
- Can words be used in different ways?
- Can words be used to make people feel better? Give some examples.
- Can words make people feel worse? Give some examples.
- Can you use the exact same words and make a person feel good or bad? Explain.
- How can words lead to a fight?
- How can you use this information to help rather than hurt people?

STICKY CELLS

TOPIC AREA: Drugs (Marijuana)

CONCEPT: Marijuana is a drug that stays in the body a long time. The specific component of that drug we will deal with is THC. This is the component of marijuana that causes many of the effects that we deem to be harmful. Short term memory loss and damage to sexual organs are just some of these effects. One of the properties of THC is that it bonds to the fat cells in a person's body. It is fat soluble rather than water soluble which is one of the reasons why it can be detected in the body for up to thirty days or more.

When we think of which organs in our bodies are made up of mostly fat cells, two are most prominent: the brain and the reproductive organs. Since these have large concentrations of fat cells, THC naturally accumulates in them. It is this accumulation that is harmful to our bodies. Since THC lasts such a long time in our bodies, even recreational users can build up quite a concentration in their system which is harmful to the organs in which they accumulate.

METHOD: Classroom activity

TIME NEEDED: 20 minutes and discussion time

MATERIALS NEEDED:
- 36 inches of masking tape for each person, plus some extra

- 6 small balloons for each team of four, plus a few extras
- A watch with a second hand

ACTIVITY: Divide your group into teams of four. Put masking tape on the floor to designate a starting line and another line opposite the starting line about fifteen feet away. Have the entire team line up behind the starting line. Give each person on the team twelve inches of masking tape. Blow up and tie six balloons per team and place them behind the line that is opposite the starting line.

Have everyone wrap the masking tape that was given to them around their hand or arm. The sticky side of the tape must be facing out. The only rule is that the tape must be wrapped somewhere below the elbow and held on by the tape itself. When everyone has their masking tape on, you may begin the activity.

They will then walk down to the balloons and try to pick up as many of them as they can by just using the masking tape. When they think they have as many balloons stuck on the masking tape as possible, they are to walk back to the starting line and then return to the balloon area. They will then remove the balloons from the tape. For every balloon that they successfully carry both ways, their team will receive one point. Any balloon that comes unstuck from the tape during their walk will not count.

As soon as one person completes getting the balloons, walking and releasing them back behind the line, they are to return to the starting line and touch the next person on the team so they may start. Be sure that each person remembers the number of balloons that they picked up and successfully carried. The round ends when all four people on the team have finished. Have them add up the number of balloons they successfully transported and report that number to the group as a whole.

For round two give them a new piece of masking tape. The one that they will have used usually loses its sticking power. They can wrap it on their arm the same way or try a new method of wrapping the tape.

For the third round there is one change. Instead of letting each person only have one chance to walk up and see how many balloons they can get, it will be a timed event. Give each team three minutes to get as many balloons transferred as possible. By adding a time limitation instead of one turn per person, the activity takes on a new dimension. They must still take turns when going to get the balloons. But now a choice must be made by the teams, are they going for quantity on each trip or are they trying to get up and back just as quickly as possible with fewer balloons? The strategy that they choose is good for discussion. Once again give them a new piece of masking tape for this round to ensure maximum sticking power.

DISCUSSION IDEAS:
- How hard was it to get the balloons to stick to your masking tape?
- How many balloons were you able to successfully carry?
- How well did your chosen method for wrapping the tape on your hand or arm work for you?

- What did you do differently in the next two rounds with the masking tape? How well did the change work for you?
- What difference did the timed round make for your team?
- How can we relate this activity to the characteristics of marijuana?
- What part of marijuana did the balloons represent?
- What part of marijuana did the masking tape represent?
- How does THC affect our body?
- What are some of the health consequences of using marijuana?
- What kind of long term health effects could marijuana have on our lives?
- What impact on your life other than ones related to the health of our bodies could the use of marijuana have?

TASTES COOL

TOPIC AREA: Tobacco

CONCEPT: The tobacco companies talk a great deal about taste when they are advertising their product. The real truth about tobacco is that it decreases the sensitivity of the mouth. Therefore a smoker does not receive the full flavor of the food that they eat. The taste buds on the tongue are very discriminating and can identify hundreds of different kinds of flavors. However, once a person starts to smoke, these taste buds are dulled and their ability to fully appreciate food is diminished. The sense of smell is also affected by smoking. Since much of our appreciation for taste or flavor comes from the smell of food, this also lowers the enjoyment of eating.

METHOD: Classroom Activity

TIME NEEDED: 15 minutes and discussion time

MATERIALS NEEDED:
- 2 Life Savers (various flavors) for each person, plus a few extras. 1 lunch sack per team
- 1 small paper cup per person
- Enough orange juice for each person to have a drink
- Masking tape
- A watch with a second hand on it.

ACTIVITY: Take a variety of flavors of candy and put about nine pieces in each sack. There should be a separate sack for each team. Unwrap the pieces of candy if they are wrapped. Use the masking tape to mark a starting line and an ending line. They should be about fifteen feet apart. Divide your group into teams of six. Explain that they will be tasting a candy Life Saver and trying to guess the flavor. Give one person from each team the paper sack and have them stand at the ending line. Have the other five players line up in a single file line behind the starting line. Assign a person on each team to keep track of their points.

Have the person with the sack take one piece of candy out of the sack, but be sure that they don't show it to anyone. To begin, have the first person in the line walk down to the person holding the candy. When they arrive, they need to close their eyes, hold their nose and open their mouth. The person with the candy puts one piece in the other's mouth. As soon as the person eating the candy thinks they know what flavor they are eating, then they are to whisper their guess in the ear of the person who gave them the candy. If they are right on the first try, the team receives one point. If they are wrong, then they must guess again. If they get it right on the second try, they get two points. If they have to guess a third time, then it is worth three points. After three tries they are not allowed to guess again.

The person who was holding the sack now goes to the end of their team's line. The person who was eating the candy becomes the sack holder and the next person in line is now the guesser. Play the game until everyone has had a turn. Keep track of how much time it takes each team. Add the number of points they scored with the amount of seconds that it took them to complete the activity and that is their total score. Low score wins.

Repeat the activity. This time have the person who will be eating the candy take a large drink of orange juice right before they eat the candy. Be sure that you keep track of the time that it takes the team to compete the round. Compare the time with the first round.

DISCUSSION IDEAS:
- How hard was it to guess the correct flavor?
- Did not being able to smell the candy have any impact on your ability to guess? Why or why not?
- How quickly were you able to guess the correct flavor?
- Which round took longer, the first or second round? Why?
- How important is flavor to your enjoyment of food? Explain.
- If you tasted less flavor, would food be less enjoyable? Explain.
- How did the orange juice affect your ability to taste the flavor?
- How can this activity relate to smoking?
- While the orange juice temporarily affects your taste buds, what does tobacco do?

TIGHTROPE

TOPIC AREAS: Depression, Suicide, Support Network

CONCEPT: Youth today deal with a great deal of stressful situations, decisions and peer pressure. Some feel that turning to others for help means that they are not strong enough to handle their own problems. Those that do turn to others for help usually choose friends who may not have the experience or knowledge to give them meaningful support. We need to encourage kids to have a strong support network to help them when the going gets rough and to have an adult who can help them when a situation arises that needs more insight than a peer can offer.

METHOD: Classroom activity

TIME NEEDED: 30 minutes and discussion time

MATERIALS NEEDED:
- Two eight foot long wooden 2 by 4's per team of ten people 3 cinder blocks per team
- 6 blindfolds per team
- A watch with a second hand
- A paper and pencil to record times

ACTIVITY: Divide your group into teams of about ten people each. Put two cinder blocks down on the ground, eight feet apart. Put another cinder block halfway between the other two. Lay two 2 by 4's side-by-side across the cinder blocks to form a long narrow walkway.

You will now have an eight inch by eight foot walkway about eight inches off of the ground.

Explain to the teams that they are to form a single file line at one end of their walkway. The object is to walk as quickly as they can from one end of the walkway to the other. They must walk using a heel-to-toe walking motion. This means that the heel of one shoe must touch the toe of the other shoe as they walk. This will keep the speeds down on the walkway and make the activity work better. They may not touch any walls, the ceiling or another person to help them walk. They must walk without any support. Stress safety as an issue with this activity.

The next person in line may not start until the person ahead of them has stepped down off of the other end of the walkway. If a person falls off of the walkway or places one foot on the ground as they walk, they must get back up on the walkway and start from where they fell from or touched. When the entire team has finished, record their time.

Now take one of the 2 by 4's off of the cinder blocks. This will leave only one 2 by 4. The walkway will now be about four inches by eight feet. This second round is conducted exactly as the first round was except using the narrower walkway. Once again record the times. Compare the times with the first round. This will be a slower round due to the narrower walkway.

For round three, explain that the person who is walking on the walkway must now be blindfolded. Once again conduct this round just like you did round two, using the narrower one board walkway. Give each team three blindfolds so the next person in line will be ready to go when it is their turn. You will need someone from each team helping with getting on and off the walkway. Also have spotters walking alongside to help in case someone falls. These spotters are not to touch anyone unless they are falling off. When someone does fall, they can be helped back on the board and start again at the same point where they fell off. Rotate these positions so everyone has a chance to walk. This will be a very slow round. Caution everyone to be careful. Record the total team time.

For round four, have the group stop and discuss how they think the process could be speeded up. The no touching rule is waived for round four. What could the team do to help each other while they are on the board? Some ideas that teams have used in the past are having two people walk on either side of the walkway and hold the walker's hands. Others have had helpers walk in front of the walker with the walker's hands on their shoulders for support. There are lots of options. Have the teams conduct this round and record their time. If time permits, have them decide on a different way that they could speed up the process and repeat this round using the new method. Once again record their times.

DISCUSSION IDEAS:
* How did you feel during round one?
* How did your team do?
* How did you feel during round two?
* What made you go slower in round two?
* How well did your team do?
* How did you feel in round three when you were blindfolded?
* How well did your team do?

- How did you feel when you had help walking?
- How did your team decide to help the walker in round four? How well did this work?
- What method did you use the second time to help the walker? How well did this work?
- How can we relate this activity to everyday life?
- What are some of the situations that we go through everyday that are not very hard on us?
- What are some situations that we go through that are somewhat harder?
- What are some situations that we go through that are hard enough that we need the help of others?
- What can happen to us if we do not have people to support us?
- What happens if the people we choose to help us are no more experienced than we are? Have you ever known someone that was going through a situation where they needed the support of someone else? Explain.
- Have you ever been a support to someone else? Explain.
- List some ways that we can support someone else.
- Who are some people that we can turn to when the support of our peers is not enough?

THE PASSING OF TIME

TOPIC AREAS: Alcohol, Drugs

CONCEPT: The use of alcohol and certain drugs affects the ability of the brain to ascertain the correct passage of time. While being able to accurately assess the passage of time may not be of the utmost importance to people, it does suggest other impaired abilities. Alcohol interferes with the brain's ability to judge events quickly and to analyze multiple situations simultaneously. This problem manifests itself when driving by reducing the ability to keep track of the many things happening as you drive down the street. Time recognition is just one of the abilities that are affected. When you cannot correctly interpret how long a car will take to travel a certain distance, you are putting yourself at risk for an accident.

METHOD: Classroom activity

TIME NEEDED: 15 minutes and discussion time

MATERIALS NEEDED:
- A watch with a second hand
- Masking tape
- 1 piece of paper
- A pen or a pencil

ACTIVITY: Divide your group into teams of four. Use masking tape to mark off a distance of about twenty feet. Have two people from each team line up single file behind one of the masking tape lines and the other two team members line up behind the opposite masking tape line. Team members should be directly across from each other. Explain that the activity involves walking in relay fashion. The first team member walks across the space between the lines and touches the next team member. That person now walks across the space and touches the next team member, etc. The participants are to use small steps. This is not a race against the other teams.

The object is for each team to stop walking whenever they think a certain period of time has passed. Everyone on the team may help in the decision as to when to stop. For example, let's say that you have given them the time of ninety seconds to shoot for. At your command each team begins to walk. When the entire team feels that ninety seconds has passed, the person who is walking at that time stops and raises his/her hand. You would then look at your watch and write down the elapsed time for that team. Do not indicate out loud how much time has passed until the last team has stopped walking. When all of the teams have finished, read out the times and see how close they came to the target time. You should repeat the activity using different times.

Be sure that you have everyone take off their watches and put them in their pockets before you begin. Also caution them to not count silently, or use any other means, to keep track of the passage of time. If the room has a clock, be sure to cover it.

DISCUSSION IDEAS:
- How well did your team do in the first round?
- How well did your team do in successive rounds?

- How difficult did you find it to correctly judge the passage of time?
- How did your team decide when to stop walking?
- What factors played a role in making your decision to stop walking?
- Did you find it easier to guess the correct time the more rounds we played? Why or why not? Is this true when you are really under the influence?
- How can alcohol or other drugs affect your thinking?
- How well could you judge time if you were under the influence?
- What are some of your other abilities that are affected by being under the influence?
- How can a person who is under the influence affect those around him/her?
- What types of activities would be harder for you if you were under the influence?
- What types of jobs would be difficult to perform if you were under the influence?
- What can this activity tell us about using alcohol and other drugs?
- What can this activity tell us about others who use alcohol and other drugs?

THE PRICE IS RIGHT

TOPIC AREA: Decision Making

CONCEPT: How much information do you need before you can make a good decision? Usually the more information you have, the better decision you can make. This activity will help point out this fact.

METHOD: Classroom activity

TIME NEEDED: 30 minutes and discussion time

MATERIALS NEEDED:
* A piece of paper and a pencil per team of two to three people
* 12 different items that have a wide range of prices. You will need to be able to show the items to your group. You can use just the empty boxes, you don't need the actual items. I have even used advertisements out of magazines and newspapers. This has included items such as the price of a rental car for a week or airfare between two cities. You will need to know the price of each item that you show.

ACTIVITY: Divide your group into teams of two to three people. Each team will need a piece of paper and a pencil. Have them number one through twelve on their paper. Explain that they will be guessing the price of the items that you will show them. Bring each item out and describe them one at a time. Give them some time to make their guess before you show them the next item. You may answer questions about the specifics of the item. Both partners must agree on the price and write down only one price between them.

Divide the activity into four rounds. Each round will have three items. At the end of each round, reveal the prices of each of the three items. For scoring purposes, give each team three points if they are within five percent of the item's actual price. They can be above or below the actual prices by five percent and still get the three points. This will allow a number of teams to receive points for each item. If you group has a hard time with math, you can write out the price spread on the board for them to use for scoring. As a bonus, you can give any team that guesses the exact price ten points. After each round (three items), stop and ask each team what their score is. Have them continue their score through the next three segments.

There is one other factor that plays into this activity. The first segment is played just as I described it above. In the second segment, you will tell them a figure that the price is below. Do not make it too close to the actual price. For example, let's say that the price of the item is $60.00. You might say that the actual price is no higher than $75.00. This way they will know that their guess should be below $75.00.

For the third segment give them an amount that the price will not be below. For example, if the actual price is $60.00 then you can tell them that the price is no lower than $50.00.

For the fourth and final segment, you will give them a range that the price will be between. If we use our same example of $60.00, then you might say that the price is between $55.00 and $68.00. This will give them a range to guess between. At the end of the fourth round, recognize the teams that have the highest scores.

DISCUSSION IDEAS:

- How well did you guess in the first round?
- How well did you guess when you were given a top price?
- How well did you guess when you were given a bottom price?
- How well did you guess when you were given both a top and a bottom price?
- Which round was the easiest for you? Explain.
- How did you solve differences regarding the price among your partners?
- How can we compare this activity to making decisions?
- How does information help you in making a decision?
- Can you always wait until you have all the information about a situation before you make a decision? Why or why not?
- How can you get the information you need?
- What kinds of people are most helpful when you need information?

THE NEWLY FRIEND GAME

TOPIC AREAS: Communication, Relationships

CONCEPT: Gathering information about people is only the beginning of a good relationship. You can know a lot of facts about someone without really knowing what makes them behave the way they do. Part of a good relationship is being able to understand what someone else is thinking and being able to successfully anticipate their behavior. Good relationships are nurtured over time, they are not the result of a one time meeting or a quick game of twenty questions.

METHOD: Classroom activity

TIME NEEDED: 25 minutes and discussion time

MATERIALS NEEDED:
- A pen or pencil for each participant
- 2 sets of questions A list of interview questions

ACTIVITY: Everyone will need to have a partner and a pen or pencil. Pass out the list of interview questions. This list should include questions such as full name, favorite foods, favorite colors, kinds of music they like, accomplishments, vacations they have taken, career goals, family members, pets, most watched TV shows, sports teams they like, hobbies, best and least liked classes in school, etc. Each person is to interview their partner and find out as much information about them as possible. These questions are only a guide. They can ask any questions that they want. Give them about fifteen minutes to complete interviewing each other. After the interviewing time is over, give them a few minutes to review their partner's answers. Now collect these sheets of papers.

Designate one partner as partner "A" and the other as partner "B". Have everyone sit in two lines facing towards each other with partners sitting opposite each other. This setup will look a lot like how you would start a game of "Red Rover", except they will be sitting down. Put all of the "A's" in one line and all of the "B's" will be in the other line. Partners must be directly across from each other. There should be about six feet between the two lines.

Explain that you are going to pass out a list of questions to each person. Tell them to leave the papers face down on their laps until you have completed all of the instructions. For round one you will give partner "A" questions that they are to answer about partner "B". Partner "B" will get the same questions, except they will be worded so that they will answer them about themselves. Give them a few minutes to answer the questions. All they will need to do is to circle their answer choices.

If you do not wish to run off the questions, you may read them aloud. Simply have everyone write down the answer that they choose on a small piece of paper. I prefer having the questions written down for them to read, but it works either way.

Here are the questions that I have used for round one. These questions were developed for junior high and high school students. You may have to adapt the questions for a different age group or a group with characteristics that would make these questions either meaningless or inappropriate. You will need to duplicate both of the following handouts for round one.

Handout for partner "A" to use in round one Questions for round one that partner "A" answers about partner "B". Answer how you think partner "B" will answer them. Circle the number of the answer you think your partner will choose.

Question #1: What will your partner most likely be doing on a Saturday afternoon?
  1. Doing homework
  2. Hanging out with friends
  3. Doing chores around the house

Question #2: What would your partner most likely drive if cost and their age were not a factor?
  1. A sports car
  2. A truck
  3. A motorcycle

Question #3: Where would your partner choose to eat dinner if someone else were going to pay for it?
  1. Pizza Hut
  2. McDonald's
  3. A fancy restaurant

Bonus Question: When your partner is riding in a car with a bunch of kids, will they wear their seat belt?
  1. Always
  2. Usually
  3. Sometimes
  4. Never

Handout for partner "B" to use in round one

Questions for round one that partner "B" answers about themselves. Circle the number of the answer that most closely describes what you would answer for each question about yourself.

Question #1: What are you most likely to be doing on a Saturday afternoon?
1. Doing homework
2. Hanging out with your friends
3. Doing chores around the house

Question #2: What would you most likely drive if cost and age were not a factor?
1. A sports car
2. A truck
3. A motorcycle

Question #3: Where would you choose to go eat dinner if someone else were going to pay for it?
1. Pizza Hut
2. McDonalds
3. A classy restaurant

Bonus Question: When you are riding in a car with a bunch of kids, will you wear your seat belt?
1. Always
2. Usually
3. Sometimes
4. Never

After you have given each person the appropriate handout, have them answer the questions by simply circling the correct answers. The partners should not try

to communicate with each other while they are answering the questions. If this becomes a problem for you,
have the lines turn their chairs around and face away
from each other. For scoring purposes, the first three
questions are worth five points each and the bonus
question is worth fifteen points. Have partner "A" keep
track of the score from round one on his/her paper.

To discover if the partners' answers match, have
partner "A" give their answer and then have partner "B"
give their answer. Do this one pair at a time. It works
best for me to walk down between the two lines and
point to partner "A" and then to partner "B" for their
answers. If they match answers, then they are awarded
the appropriate number of points. Only do one question
at a time. Go through everyone before you move on to
the next question. Read the question and the answers
to the group before you have them start answering. If
you remember the TV show "The Newlywed Game",
then you can ham it up as the M.C. Have fun with this
part. When you have finished with all four questions in
round one, ask each pair for their total score.

Now it is on to round two. You will need two new
handouts. This time partner "B" will answer questions
about partner "A" while partner "A" will answer the
same questions about themselves.

Handout for partner "B" to use in round two.

Questions for round two that partner "B" answers
about partner "A". Answer how you think partner "A"
will answer them. Circle the number of the answer you
think your partner will choose.

Question #1: What sport would your partner like to watch in person?
1. Hockey
2. Baseball
3. Mud Wrestling

Question #2: What type of concert would your partner most likely attend?
1. Country
2. Rock and Roll
3. Rap

Question #3: What kind of parent do you think your partner will be if they have kids?
1. Superman/Superwoman, who knows it all and does it all
2. Godzilla, who keeps them in line
3. A Genie, who grants their every wish

Bonus Question: Your partner has started dating. Will they kiss their date?
1. The first time they go out
2. Not until they have been out a few times
3. They will wait until the other person asks them to

Handout for partner "A" to use in round two

Questions for round two that partner "A" answers about themselves. Circle the number of the answer that most closely describes what you would answer for each question about yourself.

Question #1: What sport would you like to watch in person?

1. Hockey
2. Baseball
3. Mud Wrestling

Question #2: What type of concert would you most likely attend?
1. Country
2. Rock and Roll
3. Rap

Question #3: What kind of a parent do you think you will be if you have kids?
1. Superman/Superwoman, who knows it all and does it all
2. Godzilla, who keeps them in line
3. A Genie, who grants their every wish

Bonus Question: You have started dating. Will you kiss your date?
1. The first time you go out
2. Not until you have been out a few times
3. You will wait until the other person asks you to

After both partners have completed answering the questions, complete round two just as you did round one. After the round is over, you can combine the scores from round one and two to see which teams knew each other the best.

DISCUSSION IDEAS:

- How hard was it to answer the questions your partner asked?
- Did you ask any questions that were not on the interview list? If so, what did you ask?
- How well did you get to know your partner?

- How well did you do during the game when you had to answer questions about your partner?
- If you were able to do the interview over again, what would you do differently?
- How easy is it to figure out someone else's answer? Explain.
- What would have made it easier for you to correctly guess what they were going to answer?
- How can this activity relate to your relationships with others?
- What are some of the things that you do to get to know each other better?
- How would knowing each other better help you?
- How would knowing about each other keep you from getting into trouble?
- How does knowing each other help us from judging or stereotyping each other?
- How well would you do if this game was played and one of your parents was your partner?
- How would knowing your parents make for a better relationship?

The idea for this activity was suggested by Lisa Osborn. Thanks Lisa!

THE SKY'S THE LIMIT

TOPIC AREAS: Goal Setting, Working Together

CONCEPT: As we encourage kids to set goals and think about the future, we motivate them to reach for the stars. However, as we encourage them to "become all that they can be" we must also remind them that to reach these lofty goals a firm foundation must be established. If they want to be a doctor, then science might be the foundation; a professional athlete, then time must be spent practicing; if they want to be rich, then the study of business practices might be important, etc. We also need to warn them of obstacles that might get in their way and to prepare for them ahead of time.

METHOD: Classroom activity

TIME NEEDED: 20 minutes and discussion time

MATERIALS NEEDED:
- 10 empty soda pop cans for each team of four people, plus a few extra cans
- 2 large marshmallows for each team
- Masking tape
- 2 blindfolds for each team

ACTIVITY: Divide your group into teams of four. Use masking tape to create a four to five foot square for each team. Give each team ten empty soda pop cans and two large marshmallows. The task for each team is to build the tallest tower they can within a four minute time limit. The base of the tower may only be one can. The tower will therefore be built using only a single can for each level. Two team members must be blindfolded. Only the blindfolded team members can touch the cans. Positions can be rotated during the building time.

If they run out of cans, a sighted team member may go to the extra can pile and get two cans at a time to add to their tower. At no other time may a team member step outside of their masked off areas. Teams may throw their marshmallows at other towers to try to knock them down. They may not pick up a marshmallow that has been thrown and use it again. Team members may block marshmallows that are thrown at their towers. The distance you have between teams will impact the accuracy of the throws. Make it far enough to be difficult, but not impossible to hit the towers. This distance will vary depending on your group's age and abilities. If a team's tower is knocked over or falls over, they may continue to rebuild it during the four minute building time limit.

Call out time intervals so they know how long they have left to build. The towers must stand for twenty seconds after you call a stop to building. Marshmallows may not be thrown during this thirty second time period. Record how tall each team made their tower.

Repeat the activity, but allow them to use more than one can for the base and for each additional level as they build.

DISCUSSION IDEAS:
* How well did your team do in the first round?
* What role did each person on your team play in building the tower?

- Was there a leader in your group? If so, how were they chosen?
- What were some of the frustrations your group experienced?
- What impact did the marshmallows have?
- What prevented you from making the tower taller?
- What changes did you make in the second round?
- Were the changes beneficial? Explain.
- Did you get the tower taller the second round? Why or why not?
- If the tower was shorter in the second round, what other benefits did it have over your first tower?
- What comparison could this activity have to goal setting?
- How can we relate the use of more cans for the base to reaching our goals?
- Is it better to have a really hard goal or one that is easily reached? Explain.
- What can help us reach our goals?
- Who can help us reach our goals?
- What should we do when obstacles are thrown at us while trying to reach our goals?
- What kinds of obstacles might we encounter?

TWO PLUS TWO

TOPIC AREAS: Diversity, Self-Esteem

CONCEPT: Each individual is unique, has something to offer and plays an important role in our society. It is this uniqueness that we need to recognize. Each person brings skills and attributes unique to that person to various situations. It is by adding together these characteristics and abilities that the diversity we need to solve problems is found. We need to recognize that the diversity we have around us makes our lives and society better, not worse. By recognizing the uniqueness of each person, we celebrate how special they are.

METHOD: Classroom activity

TIME NEEDED: 20 minutes and discussion time

MATERIALS NEEDED:
- One ruler for each team of 5 people
- One pencil for each team
- One blank piece of paper for each team

ACTIVITY: Divide your group into teams of approximately five members each. Give each team a ruler, piece of paper and a pencil. Select a recorder for each group. Explain that you will read out a list of things to measure. They are to measure the indicated items of each team member and add them together to make a team score. All distances should be rounded to the nearest half inch for easier adding. After each question, stop and ask each team what their total measurement was for that question.

1. Measure the length of each team member's left shoe.

2. Measure the distance from the tip of the thumb to the tip of the little finger when the fingers are spread out just as far as they will go.

3. Measure the distance from the bottom of the knee cap to the floor.

4. Measure the distance from the elbow to the end of the little finger.

5. Measure the distance across the middle knuckles, from one side of the hand to the other. (Measure to the nearest quarter of an inch)

6. Measure the distance across the eyes, from the outside edge of one eye to the outside edge of the other eye. (Measure to the nearest quarter of an inch)

Other measurement options may be used to replace those above or to add additional ones.

Be sure the teams have added the scores from all of the questions together to form one final team score. Now have each team divide the total team score of all the questions by the number of people on the team. Total up all the team scores and divide by the number of teams to get a team average. Acknowledge the team with the highest score, the lowest score and the score closest to the team average.

DISCUSSION IDEAS:

- Which team was it better to be, the team with the highest score, the team with the lowest score or the team with the score closest to the average score? Explain. (Actually it doesn't matter, all the scores are equally important)
- Which person on your team was the most important person? Why?
- Which person on your team was the least important? Why?
- How much control do people have over their height? Explain.
- Do you have any friends that wish they were taller or shorter? Why do they wish that?
- How would our world be if we were all the same size?
- How do the differences help make our world a better place?
- Should we judge other people by how tall or short they are? Why or why not?
- How does the way a person looks affect the way they feel about themselves?
- Should we judge different ethnic groups by the way they look? Why or why not?
- Should we judge people by their religion, physical handicaps, type of family they come from or other external characteristics? Why or why not?

QUICK SHAPES

TOPIC AREA: Communication

CONCEPT: There are many ways to communicate. Verbal expression is just one of them. Much of the information that we give to other people is done not with our words, but with other forms of communication. We need to be aware that our message is much more than just the words we use.

METHOD: Classroom activity

TIME NEEDED: 20 minutes and discussion time

MATERIALS NEEDED:
- A lump of clay or play dough for each team of five
- A list of words for them to shape
- Recipe for making your own play dough:
  2 cups of flour
  1 cup of salt
  2 cups of water
  4 tablespoons of cooking oil
  4 teaspoons of cream of tartar
  Add food coloring if you want color

  Cook until it makes a ball. You must stir constantly. It only takes a short time. This recipe makes enough dough for about five teams.

ACTIVITY: Divide your group into teams of five. It is best if they do this activity on the floor or at separate tables. Give each team a lump of clay. Have one person from each group join you in the middle of the room. You will quietly tell them what the shape is that you want them to create. They will then go back to their group and create that shape out of the clay. The rest of the group will try to guess what the shape is that they have created. *They may not use any actions, words or sounds to help the group guess the shape they are creating.* (Basically you are using the same rules that you would use to play Pictionary.)

As soon as the shape has been guessed, the group sends a different person up to you. Since each group may be on a different word, have the person whisper to you the shape that they just guessed and you will whisper back to them the next shape that they have to create. That person goes back to the group and begins to shape the clay. This continues until they have created and guessed all of the shapes for that round. You should have enough words in each round for everyone to have a turn creating a shape. Remember to let all the groups complete the round before going on to another round.

Some suggested words:
snake, snowman, donut, canoe, star, tree, house, hot dog, airplane, eyeglasses, shovel, book, telephone pole, light bulb, hammer, dog bone, hat.

VARIATION: This can also be done one word at a time. Tell one shaper from each team a word and have all the teams guess the same word. Then have each team send a representative up for the next word.

DISCUSSION IDEAS:
• How hard was this activity?

- What difficulties did you have when it was your turn to shape the word?
- What difficulties did you have when you were guessing the shapes?
- How can this activity relate to communication?
- What problems do you sometimes find when people are trying to tell you something?
- What happens when the communication is not clear?
- In what ways do we communicate other than the use of words?
- If someone was telling you one thing and his/her body was telling you something else, which would you believe - the words or the body? Explain.
- Can we become confused when the words are different than the body language? Explain.

QUICK TIE

TOPIC AREAS: Violence, Personal Responsibility

CONCEPT: Many times our youth are more concerned with what others are doing rather than with what they are doing. Arguments and disagreements seem to erupt over how someone else is acting rather than being concerned with one's own behavior. How we react to various situations is the only thing that we can control. We can not control the behavior of others, but we can control our own thoughts and how we react to the behavior of others. We should understand that by taking care of ourselves rather than others, we can stay out of trouble and reduce our own problems. This we will lead to happier and less stressful lives.

METHOD: Classroom activity

TIME NEEDED: 15 minutes and discussion time

MATERIALS NEEDED: A watch with a second hand

ACTIVITY: Have everyone take off their shoes and put them in a pile in the middle of the room. Have them stand in a circle about ten feet away from the shoes. At your signal, they are to find their shoes and put them back on their feet. The shoes must be tied or fastened. As they are doing this, you call out the time that has elapsed. Have each person remember how many seconds it took them to find and put on their shoes.

For round number two, once again have everyone take off their shoes and pile them in the middle of the room. Now have everyone find a partner. Have them decide which of the two of them are taller. When you signal to begin, have the taller of the two go find their partner's shoes and come back and put them on their partner's feet. Just as before, they must be tied or fastened. You will again be calling out times so they can see how long it takes them to accomplish this task. When everyone has finished, start the watch again and repeat this part of the activity with the other partner finding the shoes and putting them on his/her partner.

DISCUSSION IDEAS:
• How long did it take you to find and put on your own shoes?
• How long did it take you to find and put on your partner's shoes?
• Did you have any difficulty finding your own shoes? Why or why not?
• Did you have any difficulty finding your partner's shoes? Why or why not?
• Could you have walked all day with your shoes tied in the manner that your partner tied them? Did they end up too loose or too tight?
• Which took more time, dealing with your own shoes or your partner's shoes?
• Is it easier to take care of our own problems or the problems of someone else?
• How well do you know what you are thinking and feeling?
• How well do you know what someone else is thinking and feeling?
• How easy is it to misunderstand what someone else is thinking and feeling?

- Have you ever known someone to react to what they thought someone else was thinking only to find out later that wasn't what they were thinking at all? Describe that situation.
- How can we know what someone else is thinking?
- Whose thoughts do we have the most control over, our own or someone else's?
- Whose behavior do we have the most control over, our own or someone else's?
- How could fights be avoided if we spent more time with our own thoughts and less time worrying about what someone else was thinking or saying?
- How do thoughts lead to behavior?
- How can we control our behavior through controlling our thoughts?

YOU BE THE JUDGE

TOPIC AREAS: Tobacco, Peer Pressure, Advertising

CONCEPT: Why do kids start to smoke in the first place? What influences them to think that smoking is the thing to do? Which influences are the most powerful and why? If we can get kids to critically look at these issues before they start to smoke, at least they won't be conned by outside pressures or interests. By taking an unbiased look at the influences around them, they can make an informed choice rather than just following the herd.

METHOD: Classroom activity

TIME NEEDED: 20 minutes and discussion time

MATERIALS NEEDED:
- A copy of the story for each person
- A pen or pencil for each group of three or four

ACTIVITY: Divide your group into teams of three or four. Give each person a copy of the story "MIKE'S CHOICE" along with the preceeding story information and directions. If the names are not ethnically or culturally appropriate for your area, please feel free to change them. Each group will need a pen or pencil to record their results. When the groups have finished and are reporting out their results, it would be helpful to list these results on the blackboard or large sheet of paper so a comparison between groups would be easier.

Read the story aloud while everyone follows along. After reading the story together, give them eight minutes or so to discuss their decisions. After all of the groups have finished deciding on their fines, have each group share their dollar amounts with the entire group.

STUDENT INFORMATION AND INSTRUCTIONS: Mike took a cigarette from his friend Joe and proceeded to light up. This scene is repeated over 3,000 times a day across the United States as new teenagers, both male and female, take up smoking for the first time. But what leads up to this final act? Well it starts early in life with advertising and other media messages bombarding our brains on a daily basis. Later, peer pressure and the desire to be cool play a part. Read this story and decide which factors played a role in Mike accepting the cigarette and deciding to give it a try.

MIKE'S CHOICE

Mike woke up one morning to the radio blaring out a country song all about the Marlboro Man. As he went to get ready for junior high school, he walked by a poster of Joe Camel that was thumbtacked to his wall. While Mike combed his hair he sang along with the radio, "Every little cowboy wants to sit around the campfire smoking with the big boys." It's not that this was one of his favorite songs, but he had heard it so often that he knew the words by heart. Pulling out the dresser drawer, Mike chose his Winston shirt and put it on. This was the one that his older brother had gotten tired of, but it still had a lot of good days left in it. Mike always felt older in this shirt since it made him feel like a high school kid.

On the way to school, Mike walked by sign after sign advertising dozens of kinds of cigarettes. Some of the ads showed a race car screaming down the track with the name of a cigarette painted across the front. There were also billboards that showed guys surrounded by beautiful girls out having fun at the beach or in the mountains. Of course many of the people that were having the fun were also holding a cigarette in their hand.

As Mike neared school, there were a couple of groups of cool older guys hanging out. They were laughing and trying to go over a jump on their skateboards. He knew some of the kids from when he went to the local fast food joints with his brother. As he stopped, one of them came over and offered him a drag on his cigarette. Mike said "No." He didn't know these guys that well and didn't want to get into trouble. Mike wished he could stay and watch longer, but his junior high school was past the high school and he was already cutting it close for first period.

After school Mike and his friends went to the store to get a Coke and some fries. While inside, they stood around a display of cigarettes. Some of his buddies distracted the store owner and one of Mike's friends stuffed a pack into his jacket and walked out. The owner didn't notice, but even if he did, he probably wouldn't have said anything since the cigarette companies reimburse him for any stolen cigarettes. The big companies figure that this is a good way to get younger kids hooked on their product. At some events they give away thousands of cigarettes just to get people started using their product.

While the group is standing around the back of the store, the kid with the cigarettes pulls them out of his jacket and offers them around. Mike had never tried smoking before and wasn't ready to start now. He said,

"No thanks." His buddies started to tease him for being such a baby. Mike countered with the fact that he was going out for track and didn't want to get into any trouble that would keep him off the team. Ryan, his best friend, said, "No one is going to know. Come on and just give it a try." Mike tried once more, "My Mom will smell it on me and I'll be grounded for life." That made the teasing even worse with Mike being called a "Momma's boy" and other mean comments. With the names ringing in his ears, Mike reached out for a cigarette and said, "Maybe you're right. Just one probably won't hurt me. OK Give me one."

YOUR TEAM'S ASSIGNMENT:

You are the judges. You are going to hand out a total of $1,000 in fines. The fines will go to the different factors that influenced Mike to try smoking for the first time. You may assign the $1,000 in any amounts you wish to any of the groups listed below. Every group does not need to be fined. There is also no certain amount that must be used for any group, but you must use all $1,000. Everyone in your group must agree to the dollar amounts assigned. Be ready to share your reason for each amount.

Here are the groups or influences to which you may assign dollar amounts:
- Music about smoking
- Shirts and posters which display brand names
- Store advertising
- Sports events that use cigarette companies to sponsor them
- Billboards that show people smoking and having a great time
- People that smoke who you think are cool
- Friends who smoke

DISCUSSION IDEAS:

Rather than having a list of questions for this activity, let me give you the areas that you will want to emphasize during the sharing of the assigned fines. These areas can be addressed during the reporting out of the fines or at the conclusion as you compare the various team allocations.

Talk about how advertising affects our thinking. Discuss how prevalent cigarette advertising is in our country, especially at sporting events and youth activities. Discuss how the cigarette companies use cartoon characters to advertise. Does this type of advertising make sense when companies say they are just trying to get adults to try or switch to their brand? Then of course explore the personal responsibility each one of us has to make our own decisions. When we are aware of media and peer influences, individual decisions can be more objective.

WE CAN DO THAT IN...

TOPIC AREA: Goal Setting

CONCEPT: When you set a goal, either as an individual or as a team, you begin to concentrate on that goal. This concentration usually leads to better performance and a more focused approach. When you know exactly what you are trying to accomplish, it is easier to meet the objective. Time is not lost searching around for what to do, rather it is spent on how to best reach the goal. The "how" becomes easier once the "what" has been decided.

METHOD: Classroom activity

TIME NEEDED: 25 minutes and discussion time

MATERIALS NEEDED:
- 3 tennis balls per team of 3 to 5 people
- 1 bucket or large paper grocery sack per team
- A watch with a second hand

ACTIVITY: Divide your group into even teams of three to five people. Give each team a bucket or paper sack and three tennis balls. Set a bucket or sack up about fifteen feet in front of each team. If you use a paper sack, you will need to have a team member take turns holding the sack so the tennis balls won't knock it over when the balls are thrown. This person does not move the sack, just holds the sack open.

Explain that each person on the team will throw tennis balls at the bucket until they get three of them in. However, before you begin, each team must state how long they think it will take for them to accomplish the task of having each member get three balls in the bucket. The team members may help by retrieving balls that are thrown and miss the bucket. Record each teams estimated time.

Start the activity with all of the teams beginning at once. Call out the elapsed time periodically. As each team finishes, call out and record or have them remember the time that it actually took them. After all of the teams have finished, read out the estimated times compared with the actual times.

Now repeat this activity allowing them to adjust their estimated times. See how close they can come in the second round. If time allows you can let them have a third round.

VARIATION: Do this individually rather than in teams. Increase the number to five tennis balls in the bucket when you do it individually. If you have the time, do it both ways and compare how much pressure people felt as individuals trying to reach their goal compared to when they were part of a team.

DISCUSSION IDEAS:
- How close did your team come to getting the time right the first round?
- How close did your team come to getting the time right the second round?
- What effect did the time being called out have on your team?

- What was your team's reaction when you finished before your estimated time?
- What was your team's reaction when you went over your estimated time?
- Did your team make any changes in strategy between rounds? How can we compare this activity with goal setting?
- Should we have a time limit on goals that we set?
- How does a time limit effect a goal that we are trying to accomplish?
- If you set a time limit, does this put extra pressure on you to accomplish your goal? Is this good or bad?
- When you know exactly what you are trying to accomplish does it make it easier or harder to accomplish? Explain.
- Why would setting goals be a good thing for people to do?
- Do you feel that goals help you stay away from certain behaviors such as alcohol and drug use? Why or why not?

WHAT AM I THINKING?

TOPIC AREAS: Anger, Communication, Violence

CONCEPT: If you look at why people get angry with each other, you will find that many times it is a result of misunderstanding what someone else is thinking. Much of our violence today is a result of not clearly expressing ourselves. We need to have clear communication that accurately reflects what we are thinking so others won't misinterpret our words or intentions. Making someone else guess how we feel or what we are thinking creates problems that can cause hurt feelings, anger and even physical harm.

METHOD: Classroom activity

TIME NEEDED: 15 minutes and discussion time

MATERIALS NEEDED:
- 6 feet of yarn for each team of 4 or 5
- A pair of scissors for each team
- 25-35 balloons of various colors for each team (I buy mine at Wal-Mart in bags of 100 for under $2)
- One needle or thumbtack for each team

ACTIVITY: Divide your group into teams of four or five people. Give each team a pair of scissors, 25-35 balloons of any shape (but they must be of various colors) and about six feet of yarn. Choose one person from each team to be the inspector. Take the inspectors aside so the rest of the participants cannot hear your instructions. Tell the inspectors that their team will be hand-ing them balloons. The balloons must be blown up, tied off, have a piece of yarn tied around the stem, no two balloons of the same color may be handed to the inspector one right after the other and the same person may not hand two balloons to the inspector in a row. If you feel this might be too complicated for your inspectors to remember, have these instructions written down for them to refer to. Tell the instructors that they cannot answer any questions from their team. If you feel this set of rules is too hard for your group, take out the yarn tying part. But don't make it too easy; you want them to become frustrated.

Now bring the inspectors back into the room. Explain to the teams that their assignment is to hand the balloons to their inspector in the correct manner. If the balloon is not handed to the inspector in the correct manner, then the inspector will pop the balloon with his/her pin. Each team has 25-35 balloons to hand the inspector. The inspector will place the accepted balloons on the floor by him/her to be counted at the end of the activity. The team with the most balloons accepted by the inspector is the winner. Explain that the inspector is not allowed to answer any questions. Give no further instructions except to clarify or repeat what you have already said. The object of the activity is to guess through trial and error what the correct manner is to hand a balloon to the inspector.

DISCUSSION IDEAS:
- What was the correct manner to hand a balloon to the inspector?
- How did you go about finding out what the correct manner was?
- How did you feel during the activity if you were the inspector?

- How did you feel during the activity if you were one of the workers?
- Once you figured out the correct manner, how easy was it to get your balloons accepted by the inspector?
- How did you feel if you never guessed the correct manner to give the balloons?
- Have you ever had someone expect you to do something but not give you complete instructions? Explain.
- How do you feel when someone expects you to read their mind?
- Have you ever had someone mad at you and when you ask them what is wrong, they tell you "nothing?" Give an example and tell how it made you feel.
- How do you feel when you try to guess what someone is thinking and you guess wrong and they get mad at you?
- How can unclear communication make us angry?
- What is the best way to deal with that kind of anger?
- What happens if you don't find a positive way to deal with anger?
- Is violence a suitable solution to anger? Why or why not?

WHAT'S INSIDE?

TOPIC AREAS: Decision Making, Stereotyping

CONCEPT: Making a decision or forming an opinion without sufficient information will lead to poor decisions and unfair judgments about people. The old saying "You can't tell a book by it's cover", is certainly appropriate in this situation. Before making a decision or deciding what a person is like, you need to ask questions and seek information. The more information you get, the better informed your decision will be. You should also consider the source and reliability of the information you receive. If you want correct information, then go to a source that can give it to you.

METHOD: Classroom activity

TIME NEEDED: 15 minutes and discussion time

MATERIALS NEEDED:
- 1 paper lunch sack for each person
- 1 small item to put in each lunch sack

ACTIVITY: Prepare one paper lunch sack for each person in your group. Do this by putting a different small item in each sack. The items can be anything that will fit in. Some examples would be, a pencil, a piece of chewing gum, a ping pong ball, a stapler, a roll of tape, an eraser, a doll, a toy car, etc. When I do this activity I just walk around my house and grab anything I see that will fit in the sack. You will get the items back. Seal the top of the sacks by stapling them shut.

To start the activity, line the sacks up in front of the room. Have your group get into partners. Designate an "A" partner and a "B" partner. Have "B" go and get a bag and bring it back to where the two students are sitting. Do not let "A" touch the bag. Have "B" hold onto the bag. Now have "A" go up and bring back another bag. Once again do not let "B" touch the bag that "A" has chosen.

For round one of guessing, have "A" guess what is in the bag that "B" is holding. Tell them to be as specific as possible. You want to know what the object is, the color of the object and anything special about the object. Have "A" tell his/her guess to "B". Now have "B" guess what is in the bag that "A" is holding. Have "B" tell his/her guess to "A".

For round two of guessing, let each partner feel how heavy the bag is. Do this by letting them hold the bag by the top. Once again let them each guess what they think is in the bag.

For round three of guessing, let each partner feel the shape of the object in the bag. To do this, they may hold the bag and really give it a good feel. Once again let them each guess what they think is in the bag.

For round four of guessing, let the partner open the bag and give one clue about the object that is inside to the person who is doing the guessing. Once again let them each guess what they think is in the bag.

At the end of round four, have the partners take the objects out of the bags and show each other what the objects are. Have all of the objects returned to the front of the room.

DISCUSSION IDEAS:

- How hard was it to guess your object in round number one?
- How hard was it to guess your object in round number two?
- How hard was it to guess your object in round number three?
- How hard was it to guess your object in round number four?
- In which round did you guess your object? One? Two? Three? Four? Never?
- Exactly how close did you come in guessing everything about your object? Why was it hard to guess your object in the first round?
- What made it easier to guess your object as we had more rounds?
- How can we compare this activity to making decisions?
- Who should you go to when you need more information about something?
- How would you know that this person is a good one to be seeking information from?
- How much information do you need before you make a decision?
- What can we learn from this activity about judging other people?
- How can we find out information about a person?
- How soon after we see or meet someone can we make a decision about what kind of person they are?
- What are some of the things we need to know about a person before we make a judgment about them?

The idea for this activity was suggested by Susan Griffiths. Thanks Susan!

WHOSE CHAIR IS THIS?

TOPIC AREA: Drugs (Marijuana)

CONCEPT: Short term memory loss is one of the problems that is associated with marijuana use. Problems with school work, social life and a career can all be linked to the smoking of marijuana.

METHOD: Classroom activity

TIME NEEDED: 20 minutes and discussion time

MATERIALS NEEDED:
*   1 chair for each participant

ACTIVITY: Divide into groups of eight to ten people. Have one chair for each person. Make a circle out of chairs. There should not be any empty chairs in the circle. Have everyone sit down in the circle. Appoint a leader. The leader begins the activity by slapping both hands on their knees twice, clapping twice, snapping their fingers on their right hand twice and then snapping the fingers on their left hand twice. The leader needs to establish a rhythm that everyone else in the group will follow. Not too fast and not too slow. Get everyone to follow along with the leader. Once everyone is going, the leader will call his/her own name as they snap their right hand and then the name of someone else in the circle as they snap the fingers of their left hand. With the rhythm continuing, the person whose name was called by the leader now must say his/her own name during the snapping of their right hand and then call the name of someone else in the group during the snapping of his/her left hand.

This process continues until someone goofs by not being able to say their own name, the name of someone else in the group, by saying the name of the person who just called his/her name or by messing up the clapping-snapping rhythm. When a goof is made, the round stops and the person who goofed must go to the seat just to the left of the leader. Everyone else will move clockwise one seat to fill in the empty chair. The object is to see how many people can play before a mistake is made. Play enough rounds that the group becomes comfortable with the process. If your group is capable, you can speed up the rhythm of the clapping.

Now the fun really begins. From now on as people move, the chair retains the name of the person who originally sat in it. So when people move, they must ask the person leaving that chair "What is the name of this chair?" Now when someone calls out the name of that chair, the person sitting in it must be ready to respond with the name of the chair, not their own name. For example, if the name of the chair is Eric, when the person snaps their right hand they must call out Eric (rather than their own name) and then as the left hand is snapped, the name of someone else in the circle. If they use their own name or can't respond quickly enough with a name, then a goof is recorded. If they goof, then the round stops and they go sit on the leader's left. Everyone else moves clockwise if there is an empty seat to move to. Once again, the object is to see how many people the group can get through before a mistake is made. End the activity whenever you feel the energy level has diminished.

DISCUSSION IDEAS:
- How hard was it to remember your own name?
- How hard was it to remember other names?
- How hard was it to remember the name of the chair you were sitting in?
- How important is it to be able to remember things?
- What difficulties would you have if you could not remember things?
- Which is more important: to remember things that have happened over the last two weeks or things that have happened over the last two years? Why?
- How does this activity show what can happen when a person uses marijuana?
- How can short term memory loss affect your life?
- What types of careers would be effected by short term memory loss?

BIBLIOGRAPHY AND RESOURCE LIST

Adventure Recreation, Sharon Black, Hal Hill, and Joe Palmer, Convention Press, Nashville, Tennessee, 1989.

Adventure Recreation 2, Sharon Black and Brad Smith, ConventionPress, Nashville, Tennessee, 1994.

Cooperation In The Classroom, David Johnson, Roger Johnson & Edythe Johnson Holubec, Interaction Book Co., Edina, Minnesota, 1991.

Cooperative Learning, Spencer Kagan PH.D., Resources for Teacher Inc., San Juan Capitrano, California, 1992.

Cooperation: Learning through Laughter, Charlene C. Wenc, The Americas Institute of Adlerian Studies, LTD., Chicago, Illinois, 1986.

Cowstails and Cobras II, Karl Rohnke, Kendall/Hunt Publishing Co., Dubuque, Iowa, 1989.

Creative Teaching Methods, Marlene D. LeFever, David C. Cook Publishing Co., Elgin, Illinois, 1985.

Discovery . . . Finding the Buried Treasure, Jerry Moe, Health Communications, Inc., Deerfield, Florida, 1994.

Do It! Active Learning In Youth Ministry, Thom & Joani Schultz, Group Books, Loveland, Colorado, 1989.

Drugs, Alcohol and Tobacco, Linda Meeks & Philip Heit, Meeks Heit Publishing Company Inc., Blacklick, Ohio, 1995.

Education for Sexuality and HIV/AIDS, Linda Meeks & Philip Heit, Meeks Heit Publishing Company Inc., Blacklick, Ohio, 1993.

Energizers and Icebreakers, Elizabeth Sabrinsky Foster, Ed.D., Educational Media Corporation, Minneapolis, Minnesota, 1989.

Experiential Education and the Schools, Richard Kraft & James Kielsmeier, Association for Experiential Education, Boulder, Colorado, 1986.

Games for Social and Life Skills, Tim Bond, Nichols Publishing Co., New York, 1986.

Games Trainers Play, John W. Newstrom & Edward E. Scannell, McGraw Hill Book Co., New York, N.Y., 1980.

Get'Em Talking, Mike Yaconelli and Scott Koenigsaecker, Zondervan Publishing House, Grand Rapids, Michigan, 1989.

Great Games for City Kids, Nelson E. Copeland, Jr., Zondervan Publishing House, Grand Rapids, Michingan, 1991.

Have-A-Blast Games, Editors of Group Magazine, Group Publishing, Loveland, Colorado, 1991.

How to Be Hip, Cool and Violence-Free, Linda Meeks & Philip Heit, Meeks Heit Publishing Company Inc., Blacklick, Ohio, 1995.

How To Lead Small Groups, Neal McBride, NAVPRESS, Colorado Springs, CO, 1984.

Islands of Healing, Jim Schoel, Dick Prouty & Paul Rodcliff, Project Adventure Inc, Hamilton, Massachusetts, 1988.

Kids' Power, Jerry Moe and Don Pohlman, Health Communications, Inc., Deerfield, Florida, 1989.

Leadership Training Through Gaming, Elizabeth M. Christopher & Larry E. Smith, Nichols Publishing Co., New York, 1987.

More Games Trainers Play, John W. Newstrom & Edward E. Scannell, McGraw Hill Book Co., New York, N.Y., 1983.

New Games For the Whole Family, Dale N. LeFevre, Putnam Publishing Group, New York, N.Y., 1988.

101 Support Group Activities, Martin Fleming, Johnson Institute, Minneapolis, Minnesota, 1992.

Outrageous Object Lessons, E.G. Von Trutzschler, Gospel Light Publications, Ventura, California, 1987.

Peer Counseling, Judith A. Tindall Ph.D., Accelerated Development Inc., Muncie, Indiana, 1989.

Play It!, Wayne Rice and Mike Yaconelli, Zondervan Publishing House, Grand Rapids, Michigan, 1993.

Play It Again!, Wayne Rice and Mike Yaconelli, Zondervan Publishing House, Grand Rapids, Michigan, 1993.

Playfair, Matt Weinstein and Joel Goodman, Impact Publishers, San Luis Obispo, California, 1980.

Quicksilver, Steve Butler and Karl Rohnke, Kendall/Hunt Publishing Company, Dubuque, Iowa, 1995.

Science Demonstrations for the Elementary Classroom, Dorothea Allen, Parker Publishing Co., West Nyack, N.Y., 1988.

Silver Bullets, Karl Rohnke, Kendall/Hunt Publishing Co., Dubuque, Iowa, 1984.

Skills for Living, Rosemarie S. Morganett, Research Press, Champsign, Illinois, 1990.

Still More Games Trainers Play, John W. Newstrom & Edward E. Scannell, McGraw Hill Book Co., New York, N.Y., 1991.

Substance Abuse Prevention Activities for Elementary Students, Patricia J. Gerne & Timothy A. Gerne, Prentice Hall, Edgewood Cliffs, New Jersey, 1986.

Substance Abuse Prevention Activities of Secondary Students, Patricia J. Gerne & Timothy A. Gerne, Prentice Hall, Englewood Cliffs, New Jersey, 1991.

Teaching The Bible Creatively, Bill McNabb and Steven Mabry, Zondervan Publishing House, Grand Rapids, Michigan, 1984.

Teaching To Change Lives, Howard G. Hendricks, Multnomah, Portland, Oregan, 1987.

The Theory of Experiential Education, Richard Kraft & James Kielsmeier, Association for Experiential Education, Boulder, Colorado, 1986.

Thinking, Feeling, Behaving, Ann Vernon, Research Press, Champaign, Illinois, 1989.

Totally Awesome Strategies for Teaching Health, Linda Meeks & Philip Heit, Meeks Heit Publishing Company Inc., Blacklick, Ohio, 1992.

Workplay, Carmine M. Consalvo, Organizational Design and Development Inc., King of Prussia, Pennsylvania, 1992.

TOPICAL INDEX

Visit the
Active Learning Foundation's Web Site

www.activelearning.org

The Active Learning Foundation is a non-profit corporation that is dedicated to helping individuals, families, organizations and communities help themselves through education and skill building. Tom Jackson is the founder and director of the Foundation. Here is a brief summary of what you will find there.

Speaking Information: Check here if you are considering having Tom Jackson come to do a workshop for your group or present at a conference. You will find his vita, costs, travel needs and letters of recommendation along with descriptions of the various topics that he addresses.

Activity Books: Each of Tom's activity books are described along with pricing and ordering information. Also available are the covers of each book and some sample activities.

Teacher's Corner: Check out some activities and research that might be useful.

Parent's Corner: See what activities and research might be helpful for you to use within your own family or as part of a parent training program.

Funny One Liners: Nothing here but fun stuff.

Newsletter: Here you will find the latest research concerning how kids learn and active learning. You will also find information concerning workshops, new books and other resource information.

Real Life Stories: People who work with children and youth have shared their success stories regarding active learning.

Educators, Counselors, Youth Workers and Others: *Hear Tom Jackson Live!*

That's right! Wouldn't it be great to have Tom come to your school or conference and share with you his creative, yet practical hands-on activities? Tom's activities have been described by teachers and others who work with children and youth as "Simply the best life skill activities I have ever used! They teach life skills in such a way that kids not only learn, but love doing them." Or you can broaden the topic by having Tom talk about active learning as a teaching tool which can energize any classroom or program.

Reading about the activities is exciting, but there is no substitute for experiencing them. Tom uses his "learn by doing" approach to walk you through a number of activities from his books. Here is a chance to ask questions, get insider tips and learn first hand how to process and discuss the activities with your kids. Hundreds of teachers, counselors, youth workers and others have participated in Tom's workshops, and one of the most common remarks is, "I wish we had more time. This is the most useful workshop I have ever attended."

Tom is available for keynote presentations, conference breakouts, workshops, teacher in-services, peer helper trainings, youth leadership programs and conferences. Funding sources that have been used successfully by other organizations include staff development, Safe and Drug Free Schools, Title I, At-Risk and High Risk, as well as special grants and community resources. Join up with a neighboring school, school district or organization and save money by sharing travel costs when Tom stays more than one day in your part of the country. We will even try to book another workshop in your area to help you save money on travel if you will give us other likely people to contact!

Give Janet Jackson a call at (888) 588-7078 and ask for Tom's speaker packet. Or, just give Janet a call and suggest to her a person in your school district or organization who would be interested in hearing more about Tom and she'll contact them directly.

Parents, Parenting Instructors,
Parent/School Organizations and Others
Who Are Interested In Helping Families:
Invite Tom Jackson To Your Area

Help families help themselves! Invite Tom Jackson to make a presentation to the parents in your area. Tom doesn't conduct the usual parenting workshop where someone tells parents how they should parent. Instead, he gives parents easy to do, hands-on activities that can be done right in their own homes to open up the lines of communication and discuss important topics with their children in a non-threatening way. Tom also conducts workshops specifically for parenting instructors which focuses on how to facilitate parent trainings using Tom's activities.

Explore the values of caring, cooperation, honesty, perseverance, respect, responsibility, and service to others along with other topics. Rather than telling you what to believe, the activities provide a user-friendly vehicle to allow each parent the opportunity to share their own values with their children and have fun at the same time.

Reading about an activity is exciting, but there is no substitute for experiencing them. Tom uses his "learn by doing" approach to let you participate in a number of activities from his book *Activities That Teach Family Values*. Here is a chance to ask questions, get insider tips and learn first hand how to use the activities to discuss values with your kids.

Tom is available for keynote presentations, conference breakouts, workshops and evening presentations. These can be done for parents, trainers of parents or others who work with families. Another option is to conduct a workshop for parents and their children ages 7 to 15Z\x. Have them actually experience the activities together and see how much fun they really are!

Give Janet Jackson a call at (888) 588-7078 and ask for Tom's speaker packet. Or, just give Janet a call and suggest to her a person in your school district or organization who would be interested in hearing more about Tom and she'll contact them directly.

Still More Activities That Teach: 55 all new activities which address all of the topics from previous books, along with these new topics, conflict resolution, respect, responsibility, school-to-careers, team building, media influence and healthy lifestyles. Discussion questions at the end of each activity are divided into easy-to-use categories. 257 pages. Retail price $15.95 (Case discounts available)

Activities That Teach Family Values: 52 new activities that can be used by parents, character education programs, small group sessions, church groups or after-school programs to help adults stop preaching to kids and start sharing with them instead. Once again Tom's hands-on approach is used to address topics such as caring, cooperation, honesty, perseverance, respect, responsibility, service to others and much, much more. 217 pages. $14.95 (Case discounts available)

Conducting Successful Group Discussions With Kids: A leader's guide to making an activity meaningful and educational! Discover a simple, yet effective four step discussion outline that is effective and engaging. Additional strategies include getting kids to talk, questions to ask, discussion formats to use, room arrangement, teacher tips, student behaviors and much more. 120 pages. Retail price $12.95 (Case discounts available)

For ordering information about any of Tom's books:

Call toll free (888) 588-7078 between the hours of 7:00 a.m. and 7:00 p.m. Mountain Time

Write: Active Learning Center, 3835 West 800 North,
Cedar City, UT 84720
FAX: 435-586-0185
web site: www.activelearning.org
e-mail: staff@activelearning.org
Mastercard, Visa, Checks, or Purchase Orders
gladly accepted

Other Books by Tom Jackson

Book covers and sample activities may be viewed at www.activelearning.org

Don't miss out! Be sure you have all of Tom's powerful, hands-on activities and discussion techniques which you can use immediately to make a real difference in the lives of kids. Each book has different activities in them.

These activities and discussion strategies will create excitement and increased learning anywhere there is a group of kids. Thousands of professionals have successfully used these activities with elementary and secondary groups and have found them effective with inner city, suburban, rural, high-risk and at-risk populations. These fun, hands-on activities have been tested in the real world of classrooms, after school programs, churches, prevention programs, treatment centers, juvenile detention centers, etc.

Students learn best by doing! All of Tom's activity books contain user-friendly activities that get kids involved in their own learning process and let them have fun at the same time. The books include opening chapters on how-to use activities and tips for leading effective discussions. Each activity is followed by a list of questions that can be used to help you transfer what you did during the activity to real life applications. These activities can be used in classrooms, counseling and support groups, youth programs, after school programs, churches or anywhere else you would find a group of kids. Great for all grade levels!

Activities That Teach: 60 hands-on activities that address topics such as alcohol, tobacco and drug prevention, and which teach skills related to communication, values, working together, problem solving, stress management, goal setting, self-esteem, decision making and more. 234 pages. Retail price: $15.95 (Case discounts available)